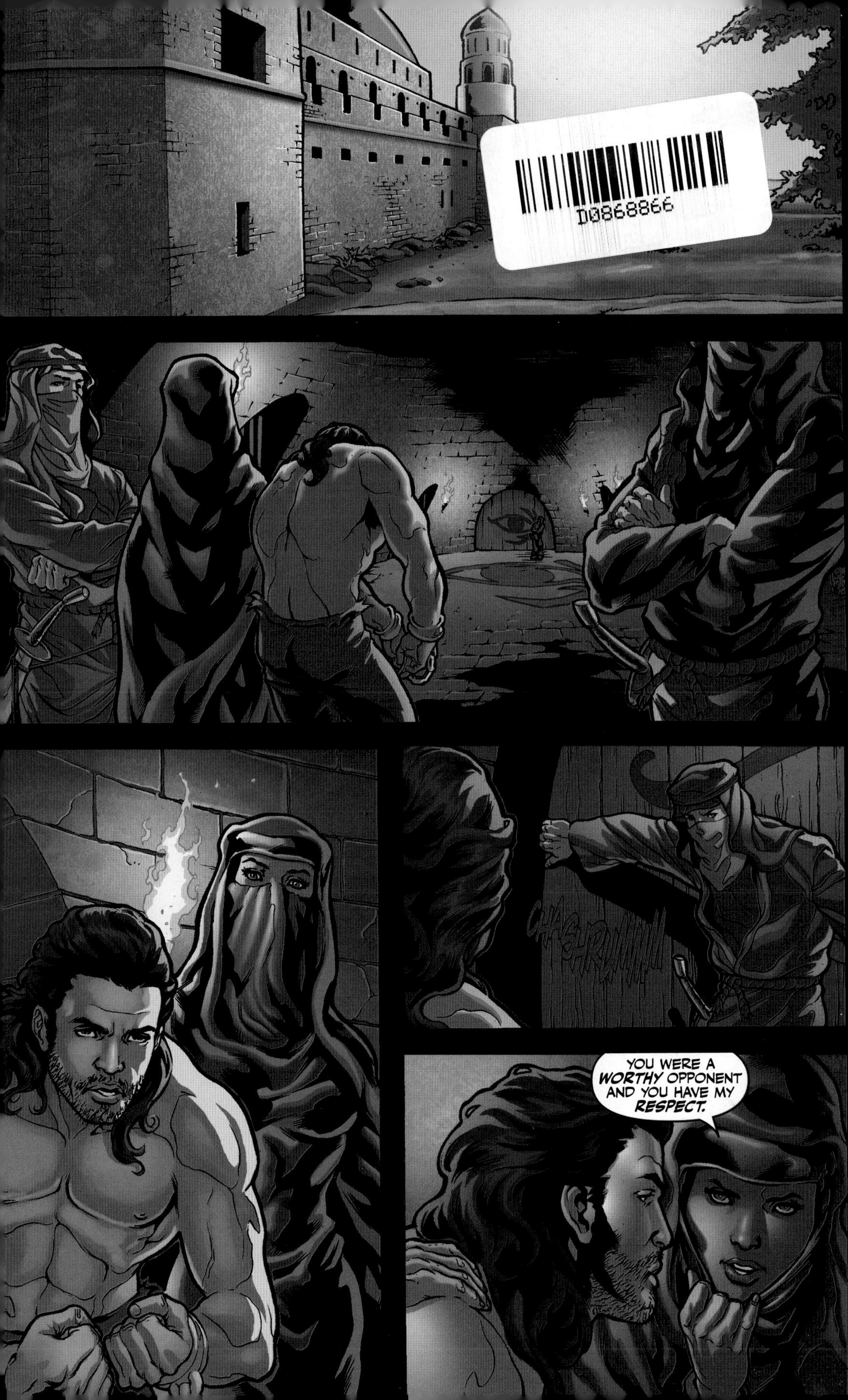
YOU WERE A *WORTHY* OPPONENT AND YOU HAVE MY *RESPECT.*

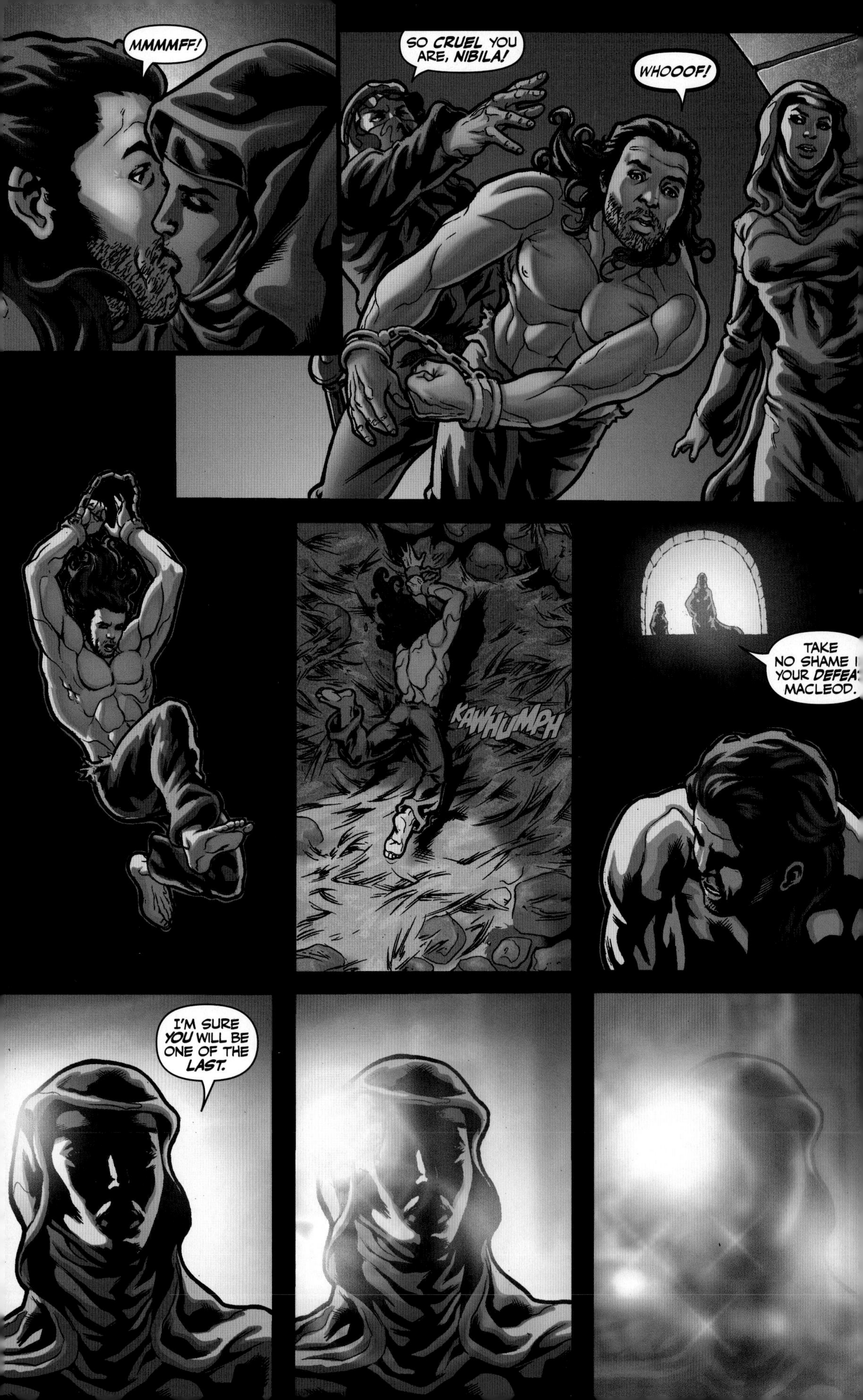
MMMMFF!
SO CRUEL YOU ARE, NIBILA!
WHOOOF!
KAWHUMPH
TAKE NO SHAME I YOUR DEFEA MACLEOD.
I'M SURE YOU WILL BE ONE OF THE LAST.

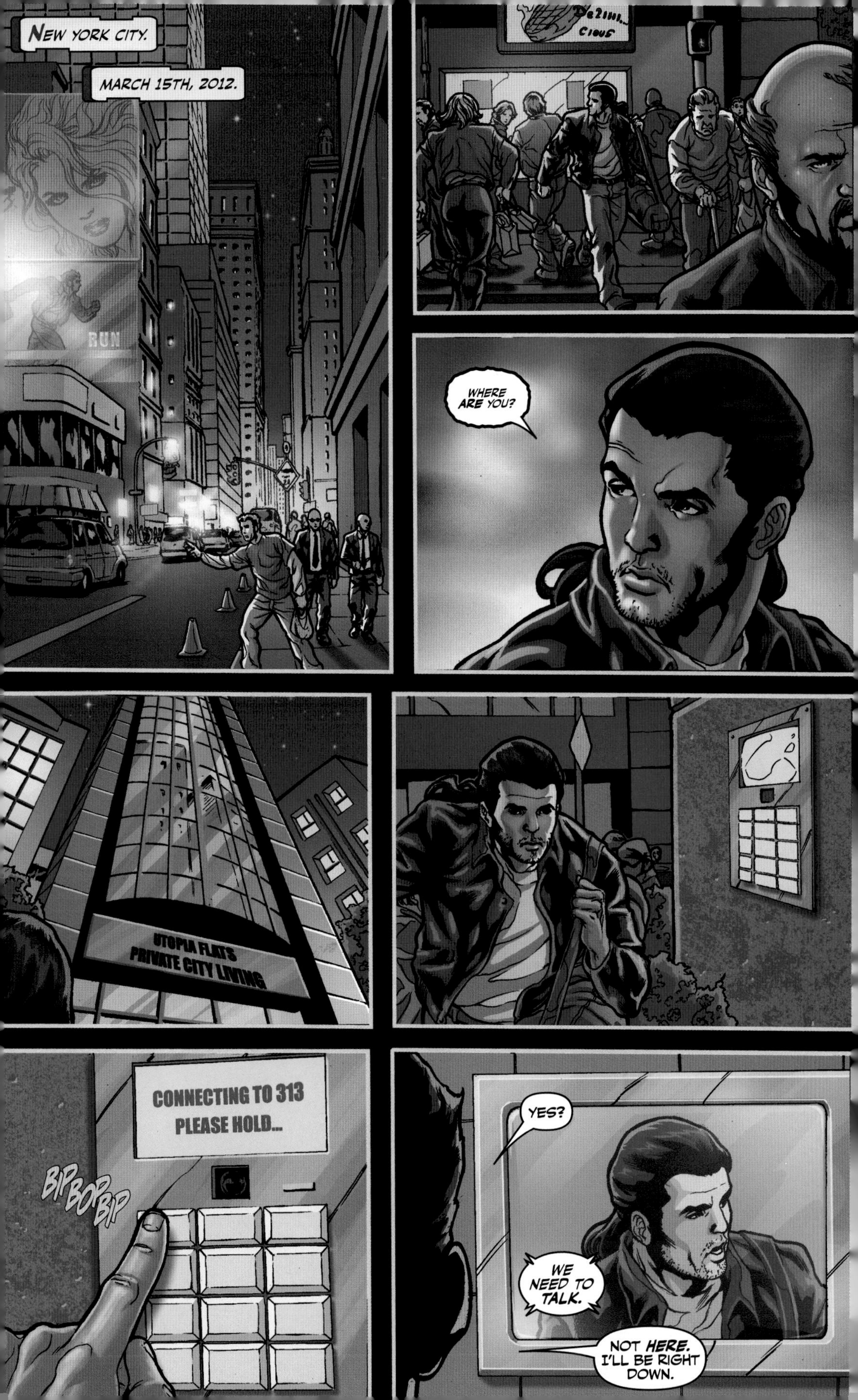
NEW YORK CITY.
MARCH 15TH, 2012.
RUN
WHERE ARE YOU?
UTOPIA FLATS
PRIVATE CITY LIVING
CONNECTING TO 313
PLEASE HOLD...
BIP BOP BIP
YES?
WE NEED TO TALK.
NOT HERE. I'LL BE RIGHT DOWN.

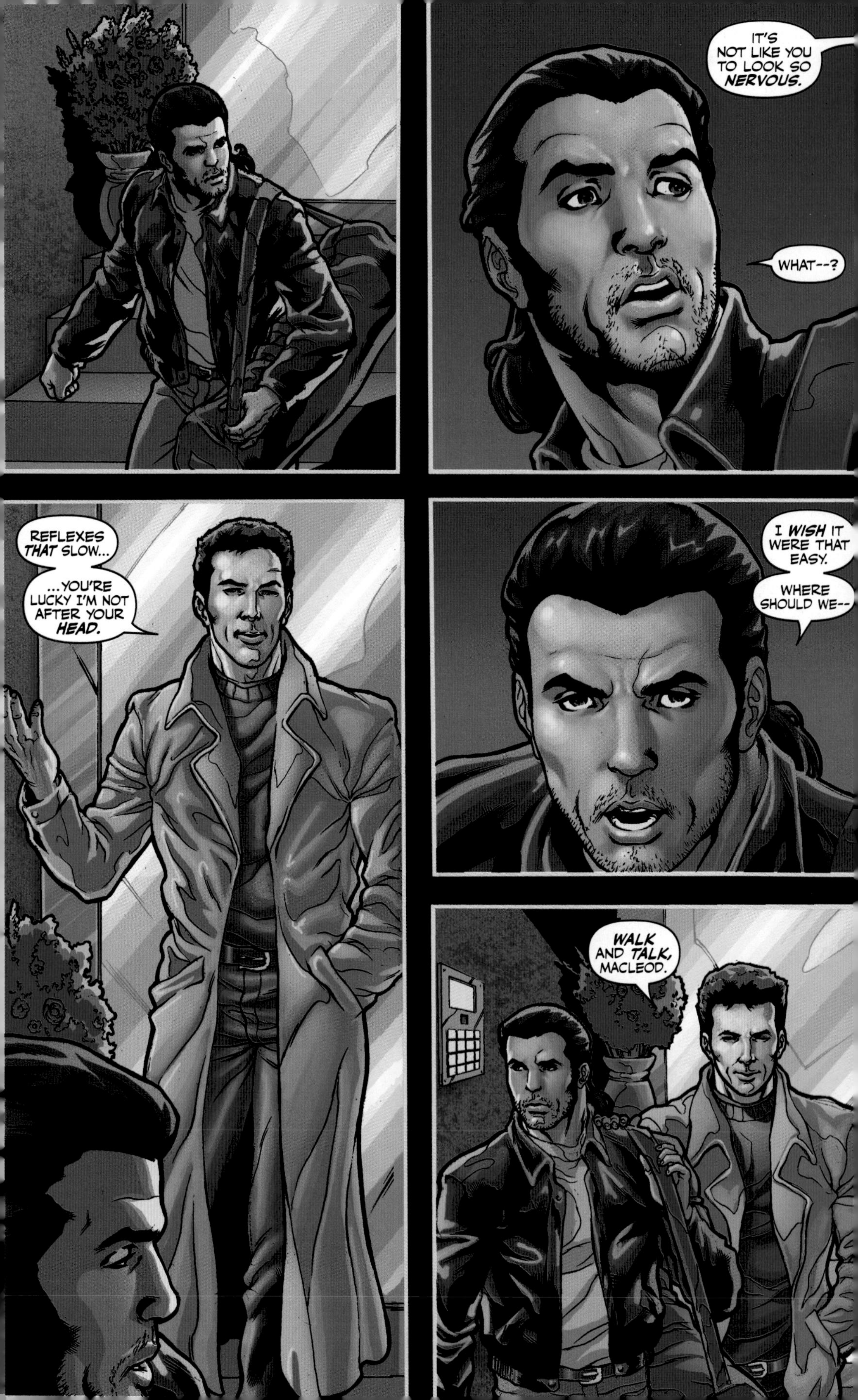
IT'S NOT LIKE YOU TO LOOK SO *NERVOUS.*
WHAT--?
REFLEXES *THAT* SLOW...
...YOU'RE LUCKY I'M NOT AFTER YOUR *HEAD.*
I *WISH* IT WERE THAT EASY.
WHERE SHOULD WE--
WALK AND *TALK,* MACLEOD.

I SUSPECT I ALREADY KNOW THE *ANSWER*, BUT LET'S ASK THE QUESTION *ANYWAY:* WHY ARE YOU HERE?

SOMETHING'S... *OFF.*

[...]BE IT'S [...], BUT IT'S [...]AN SENSE [...]ACK OF [...]CE...OUT [...] IN THE [...]HER.

[...]ON [...]HAT, I'VE [...]ARING A [...]UMORS [...]LY.

RUMORS?

CRAZY THINGS.

IMMORTAL *CONSPIRACY* THEORIES, MASS ELIMINATIONS, PEOPLE GOING *MISSING...*

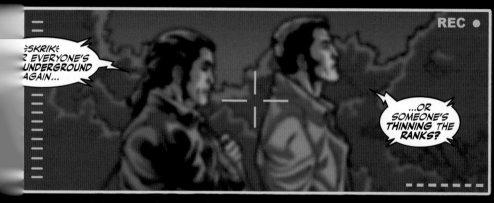

REC ●

≈SKRIK≈ [...] EVERYONE'S UNDERGROUND AGAIN...

...OR SOMEONE'S *THINNING* THE RANKS?

I'VE HEARD THE SAME RUMORS. I WASN'T SURE *WHAT* TO BELIEVE...BUT WHEN [...] STARTED HAVING TROUBLE TRACKING DOWN THE *USUAL SUSPECTS,* I STARTED TO *WORRY.*

ON THE OTHER HAND, I'M SORT OF *GLAD* TO *HEAR* I DON'T HAVE THE MARKET CORNERED ON *PARANOIA* FOR ONCE.

I HAVE A *DIGITAL FIX* ON THEM. *AUDIO* AND *VIDEO* ARE *CLEAN.*

AM I *HOLDING?*

AFFIRMATIVE, HOLD POSITION.

THE *SHOW'LL* START SOON ENOUGH.

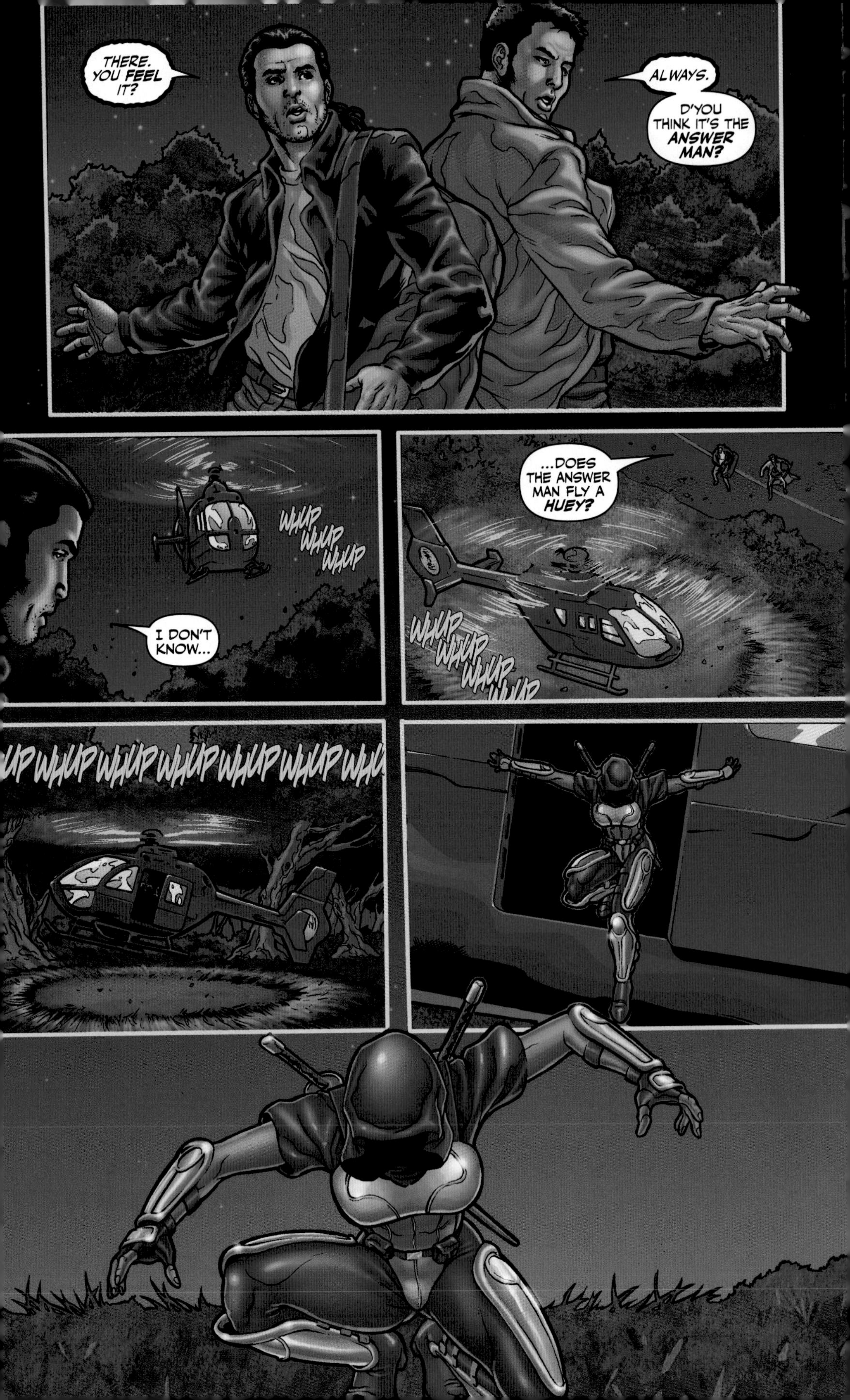
THERE. YOU FEEL IT?
ALWAYS.
D'YOU THINK IT'S THE ANSWER MAN?
WHUP WHUP WHUP
I DON'T KNOW...
...DOES THE ANSWER MAN FLY A HUEY?
WHUP WHUP WHUP
WHUP WHUP WHUP WHUP WHUP WHUP

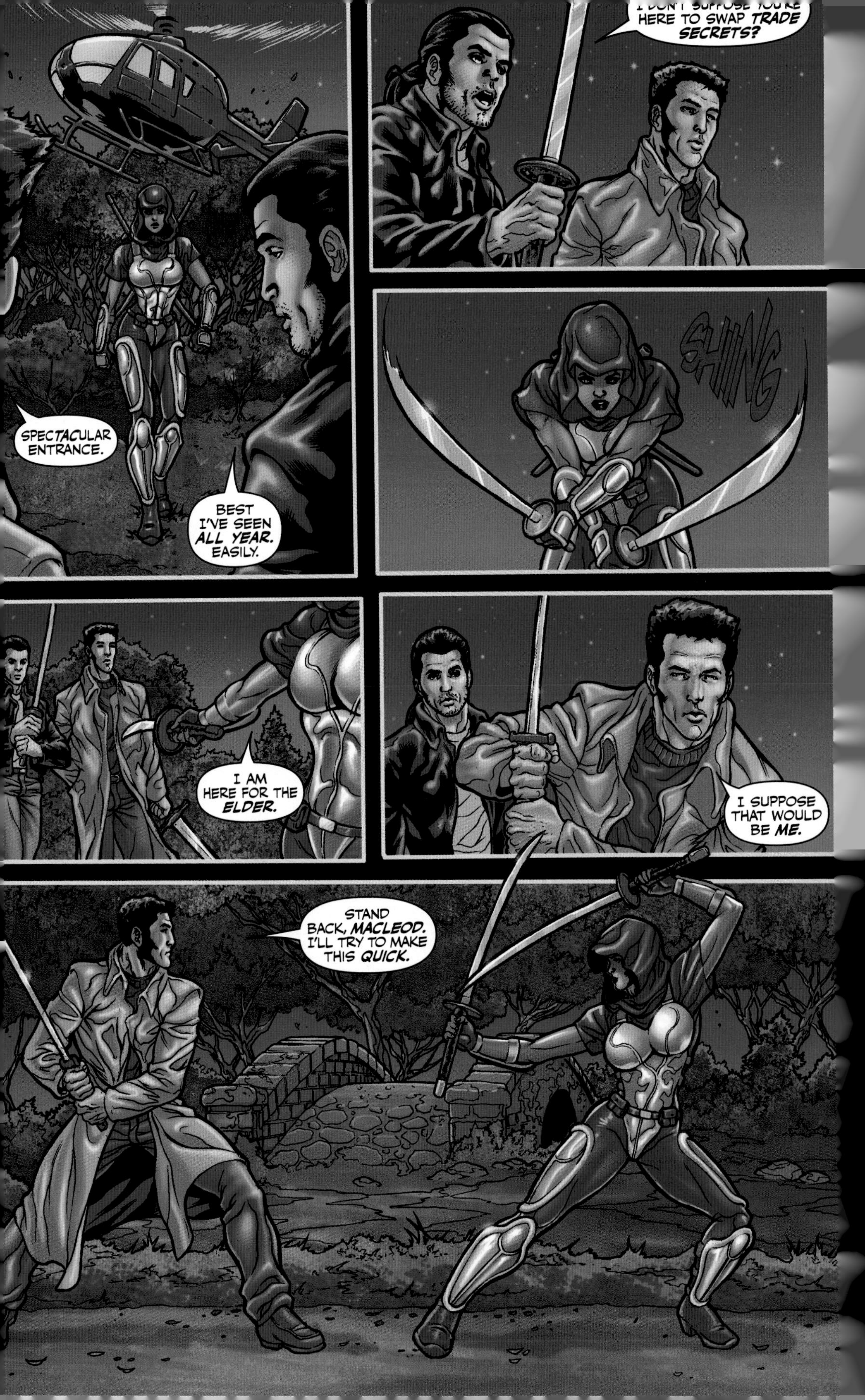
SPECTACULAR ENTRANCE.
BEST I'VE SEEN ALL YEAR. EASILY.
HERE TO SWAP TRADE SECRETS?
SHIING
I AM HERE FOR THE ELDER.
I SUPPOSE THAT WOULD BE ME.
STAND BACK, MACLEOD. I'LL TRY TO MAKE THIS QUICK.

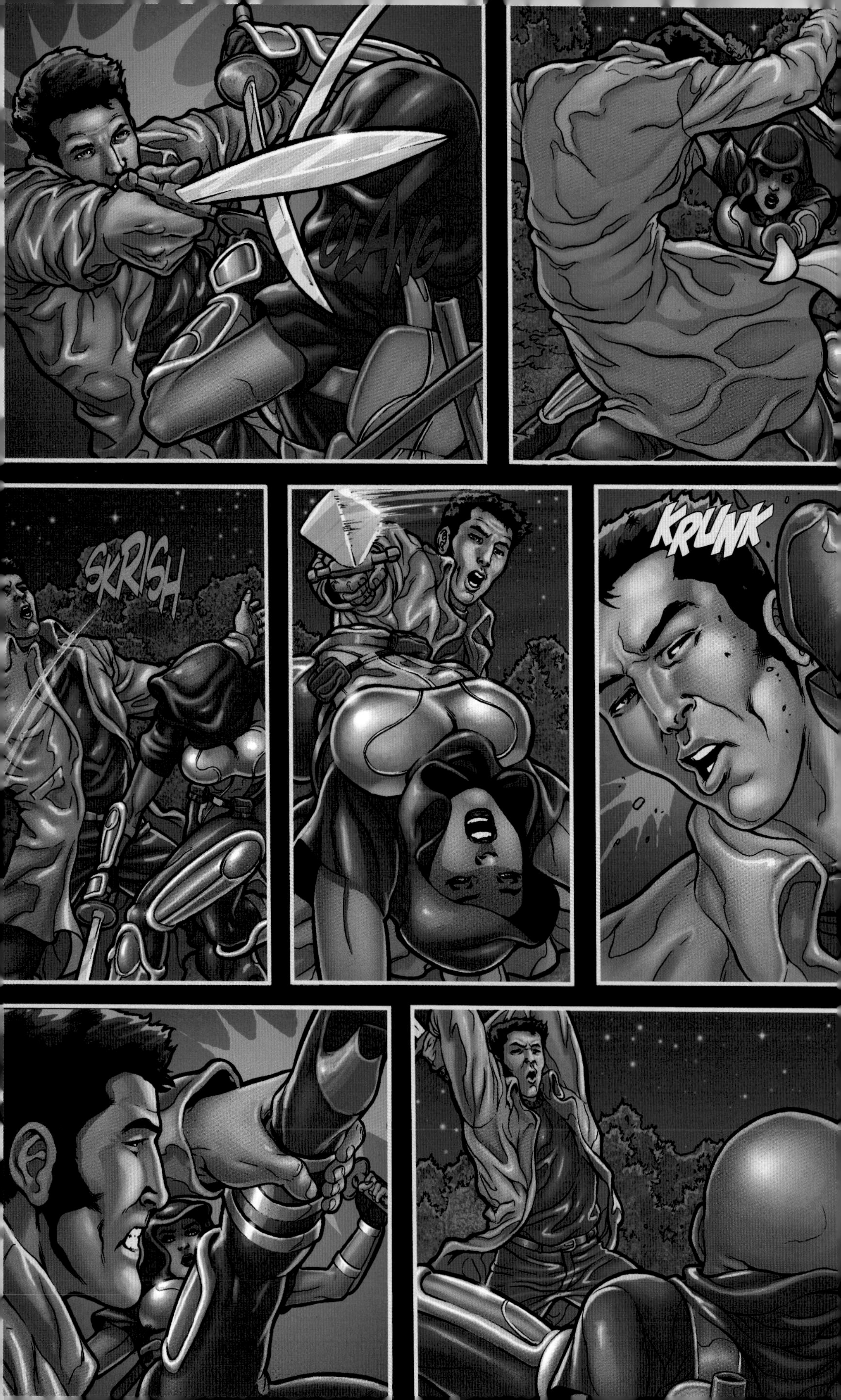

CLANG
SKRISH
KRUNK

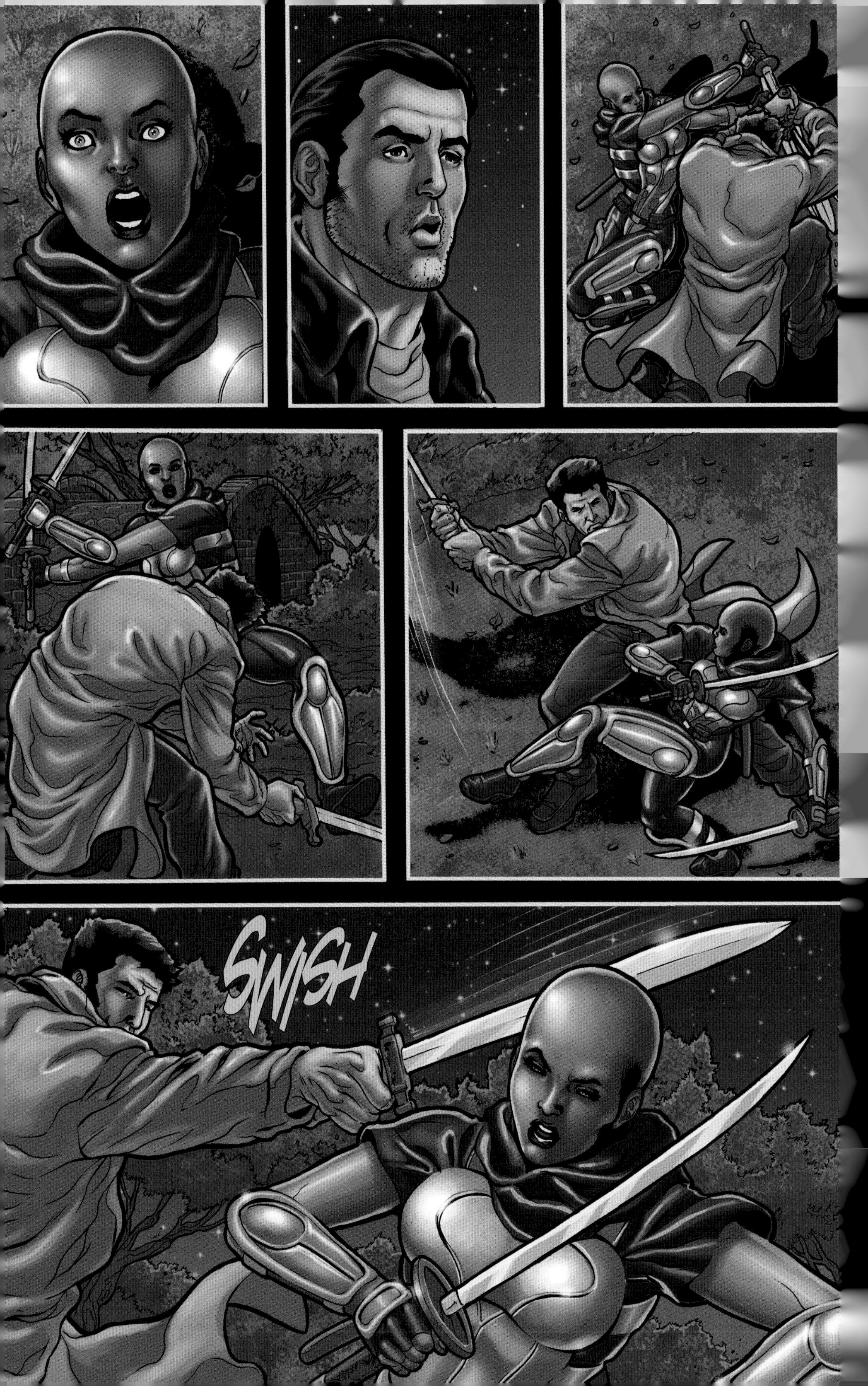
SWISH

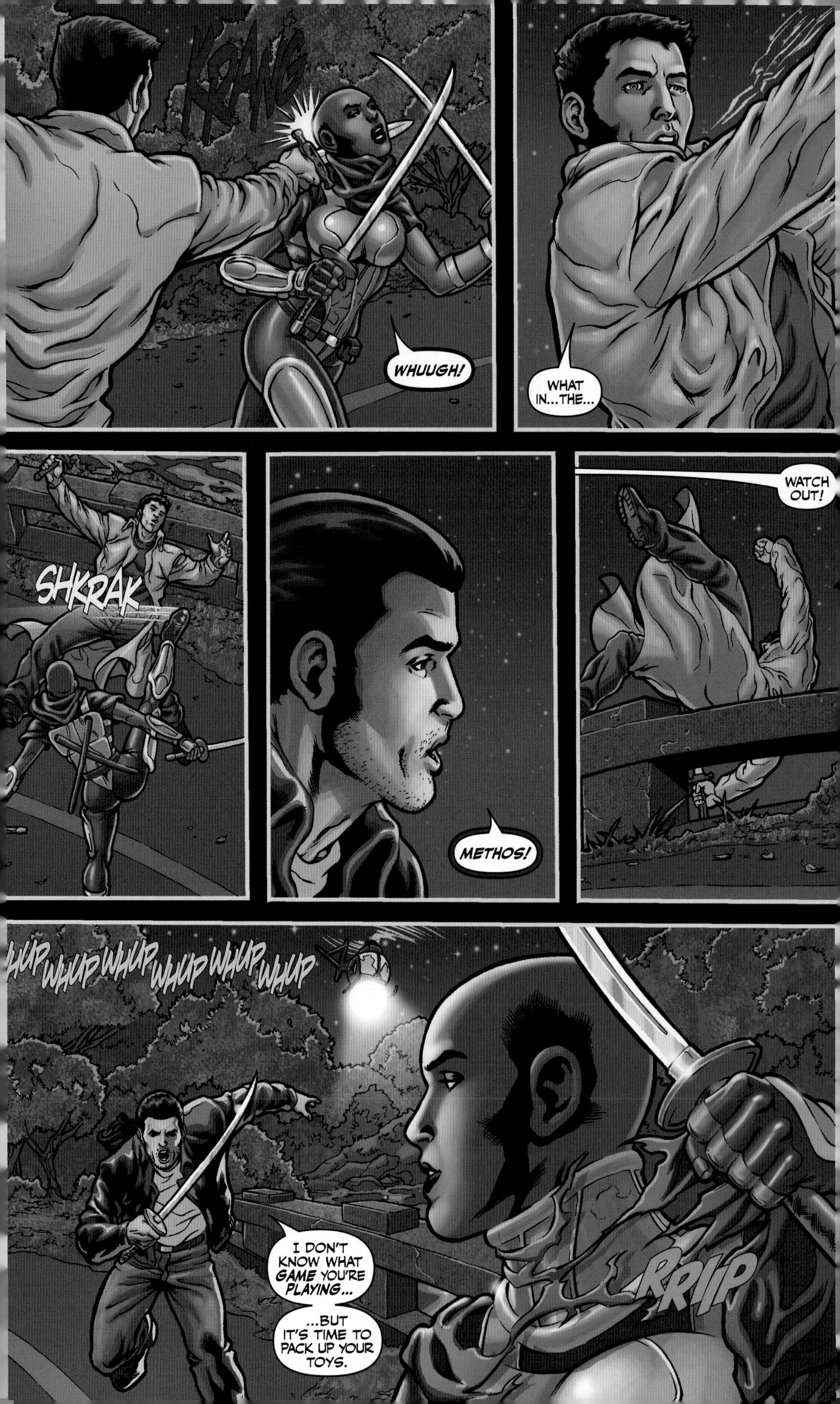
KRANG
WHUUGH!
WHAT IN...THE...
SHKRAK
METHOS!
WATCH OUT!
WHUP WHUP WHUP WHUP WHUP WHUP
I DON'T KNOW WHAT GAME YOU'RE PLAYING...
...BUT IT'S TIME TO PACK UP YOUR TOYS.
RRIP

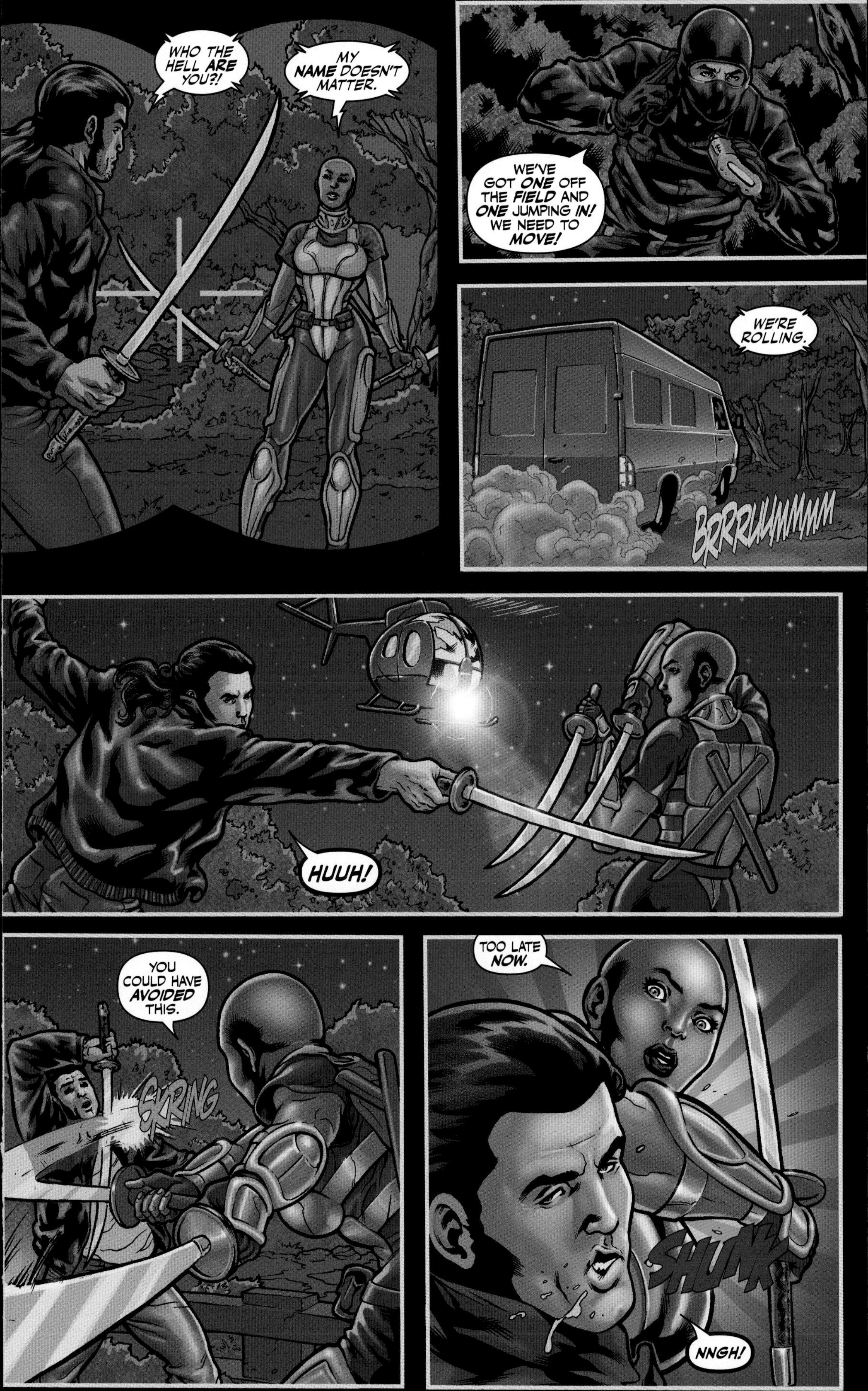
WHO THE HELL ARE YOU?!
MY NAME DOESN'T MATTER.
WE'VE GOT ONE OFF THE FIELD AND ONE JUMPING IN! WE NEED TO MOVE!
WE'RE ROLLING.
BRRRUUMMMM
HUUH!
YOU COULD HAVE AVOIDED THIS.
SKRING
TOO LATE NOW.
NNGH!

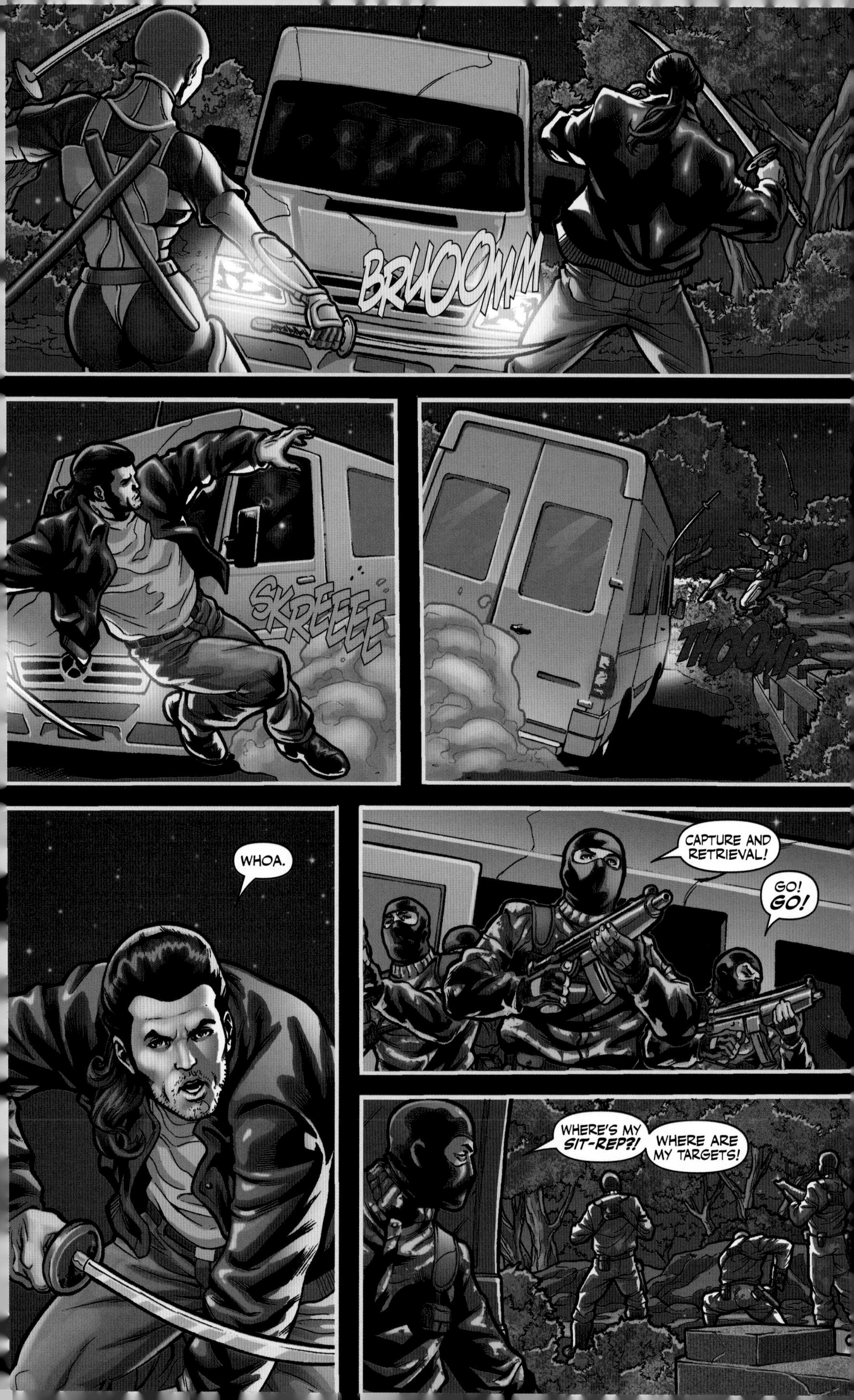
BRUOOMM
SKREEEE
THOOMP
WHOA.
CAPTURE AND RETRIEVAL!
GO! GO!
WHERE'S MY SIT-REP?!
WHERE ARE MY TARGETS!

WHUP WHUP WHUP WHUP

DOWN THERE, THEY'RE PULLING OUT.

LOOKS LIKE SHE'S TAKING HIM WITH HER.

WHAT?!

NONE OF THIS MAKES ANY SENSE.

OPEN ‚ ON THAT ! TAKE IT OUT!

LET ME GO DOWN THERE! I CAN HANDLE THIS!

BRUKKABRUKKABRUKKABRUKK

BRUKKABRUKKABRUKK

HEAVY GUN! TAKE COVER!

GET DOWN! ALL OF YOU!

HUAAGH!

BRUKKABRUKKABRUKKABRUKKABRUKKABR

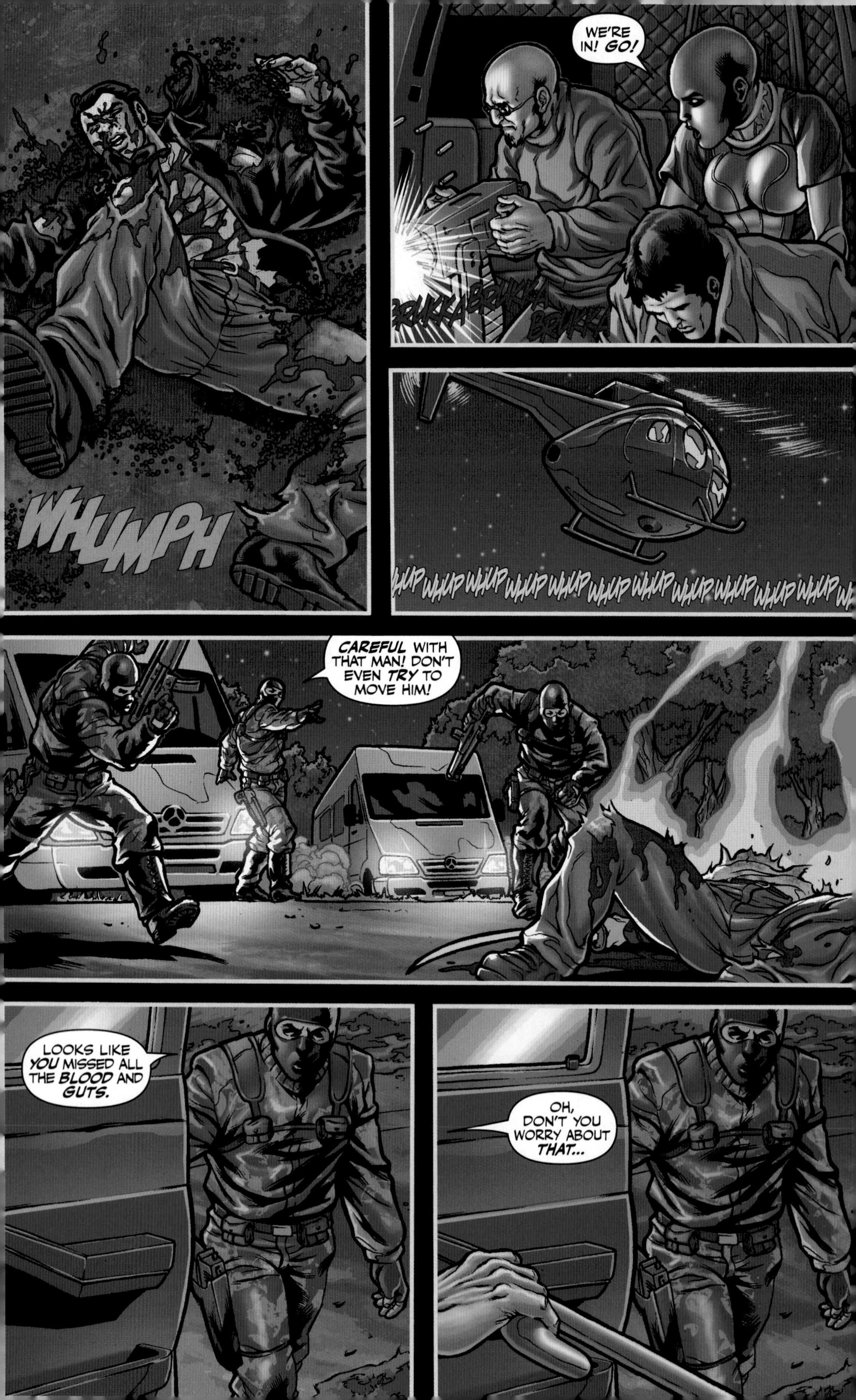
WHUMPH
WE'RE IN! GO!
BRUKKA BRUKKA BRUKKA
WHUP WHUP WHUP WHUP WHUP WHUP WHUP WHUP WHUP WHUP WHUP WHUP
CAREFUL WITH THAT MAN! DON'T EVEN TRY TO MOVE HIM!
LOOKS LIKE YOU MISSED ALL THE BLOOD AND GUTS.
OH, DON'T YOU WORRY ABOUT THAT...

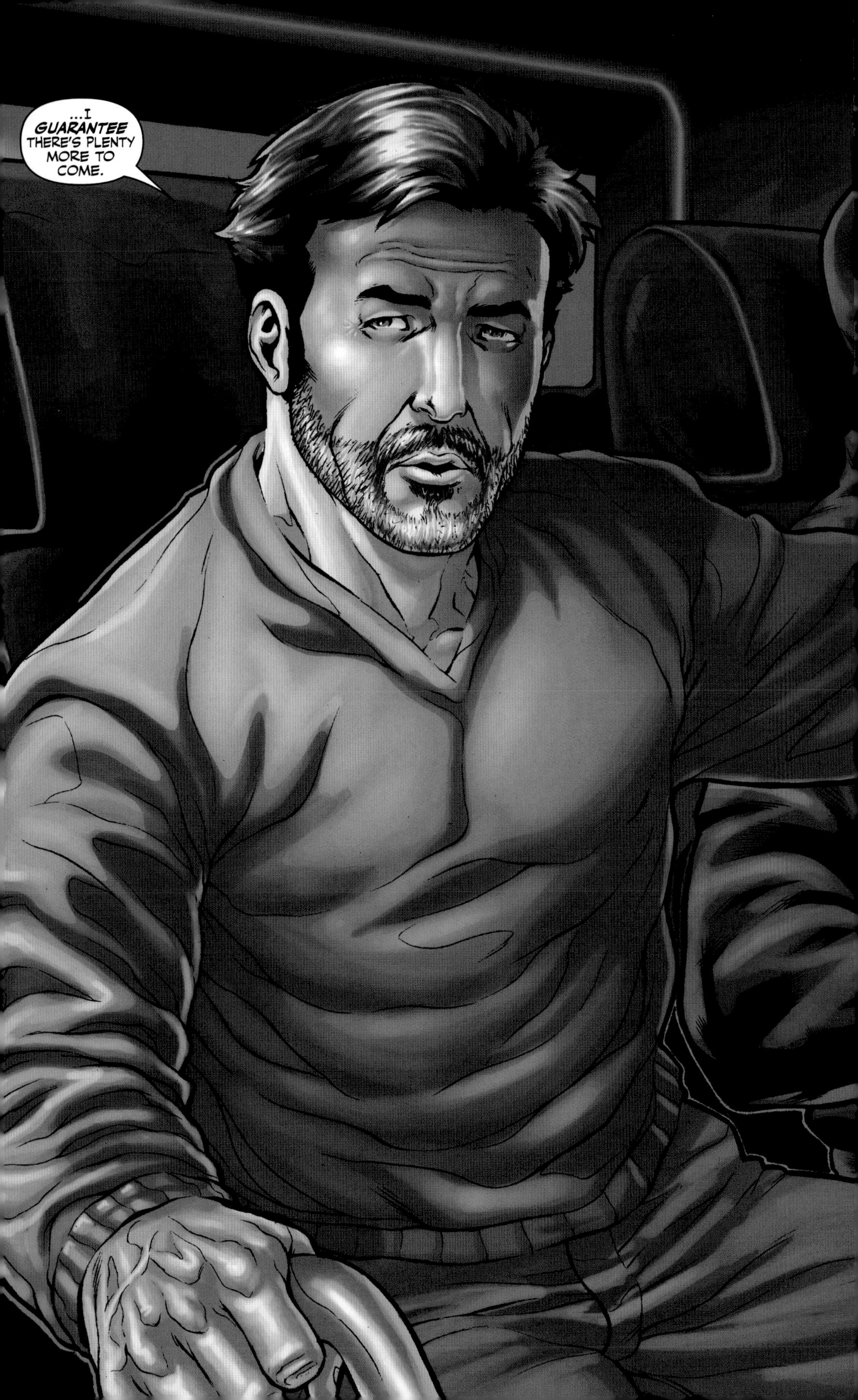
...I GUARANTEE THERE'S PLENTY MORE TO COME.

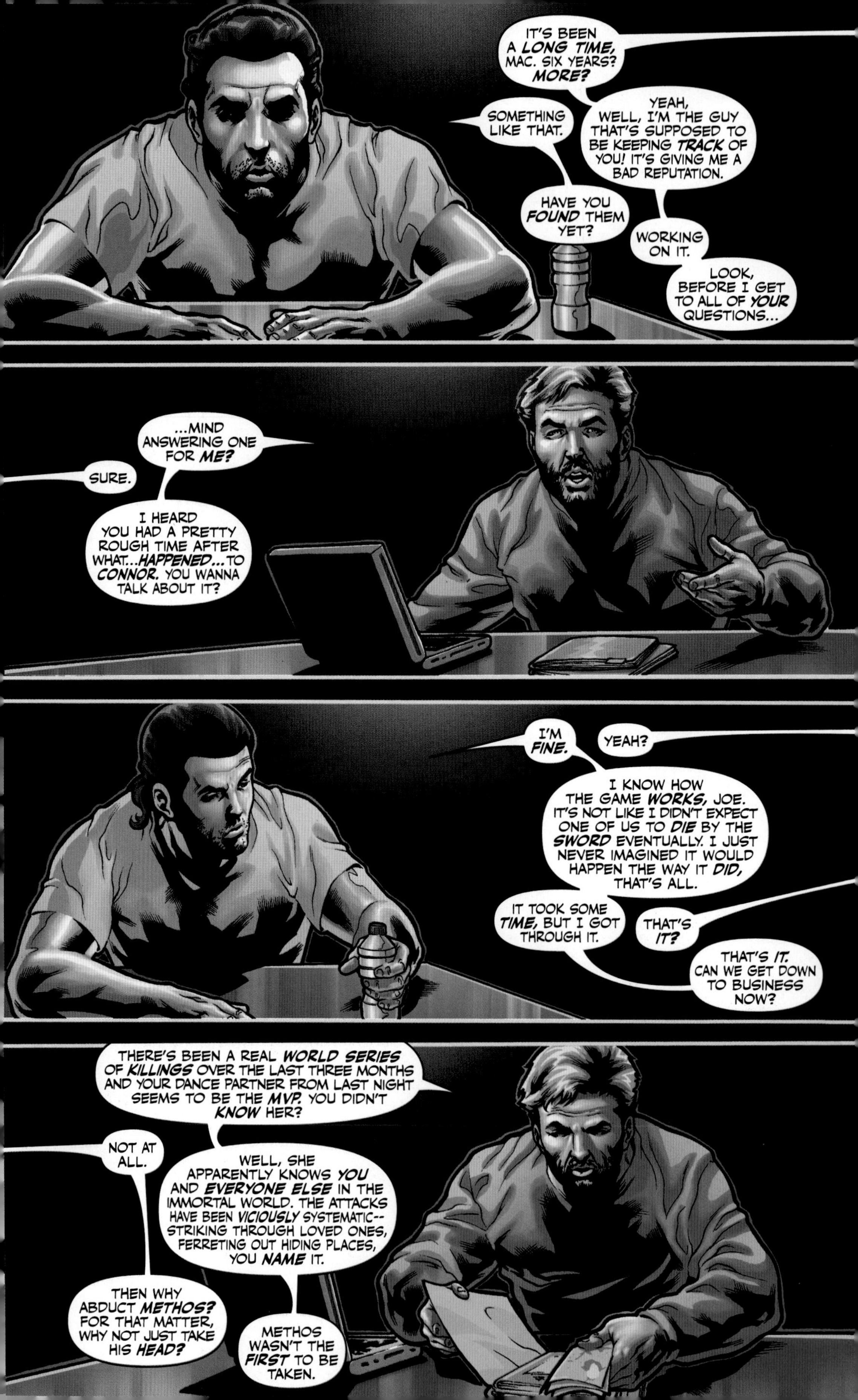

IT'S BEEN A *LONG TIME,* MAC. SIX YEARS? *MORE?*
SOMETHING LIKE THAT.
YEAH, WELL, I'M THE GUY THAT'S SUPPOSED TO BE KEEPING *TRACK* OF YOU! IT'S GIVING ME A BAD REPUTATION.
HAVE YOU *FOUND* THEM YET?
WORKING ON IT.
LOOK, BEFORE I GET TO ALL OF *YOUR* QUESTIONS...
...MIND ANSWERING ONE FOR *ME?*
SURE.
I HEARD YOU HAD A PRETTY ROUGH TIME AFTER WHAT...*HAPPENED*...TO *CONNOR.* YOU WANNA TALK ABOUT IT?
I'M *FINE.*
YEAH?
I KNOW HOW THE GAME *WORKS,* JOE. IT'S NOT LIKE I DIDN'T EXPECT ONE OF US TO *DIE* BY THE *SWORD* EVENTUALLY. I JUST NEVER IMAGINED IT WOULD HAPPEN THE WAY IT *DID,* THAT'S ALL.
IT TOOK SOME *TIME,* BUT I GOT THROUGH IT.
THAT'S *IT?*
THAT'S *IT.* CAN WE GET DOWN TO BUSINESS NOW?
THERE'S BEEN A REAL *WORLD SERIES* OF *KILLINGS* OVER THE LAST THREE MONTHS AND YOUR DANCE PARTNER FROM LAST NIGHT SEEMS TO BE THE *MVP.* YOU DIDN'T *KNOW* HER?
NOT AT ALL.
WELL, SHE APPARENTLY KNOWS *YOU* AND *EVERYONE ELSE* IN THE IMMORTAL WORLD. THE ATTACKS HAVE BEEN *VICIOUSLY* SYSTEMATIC-- STRIKING THROUGH LOVED ONES, FERRETING OUT HIDING PLACES, YOU *NAME* IT.
THEN WHY ABDUCT *METHOS?* FOR THAT MATTER, WHY NOT JUST TAKE HIS *HEAD?*
METHOS WASN'T THE *FIRST* TO BE TAKEN.

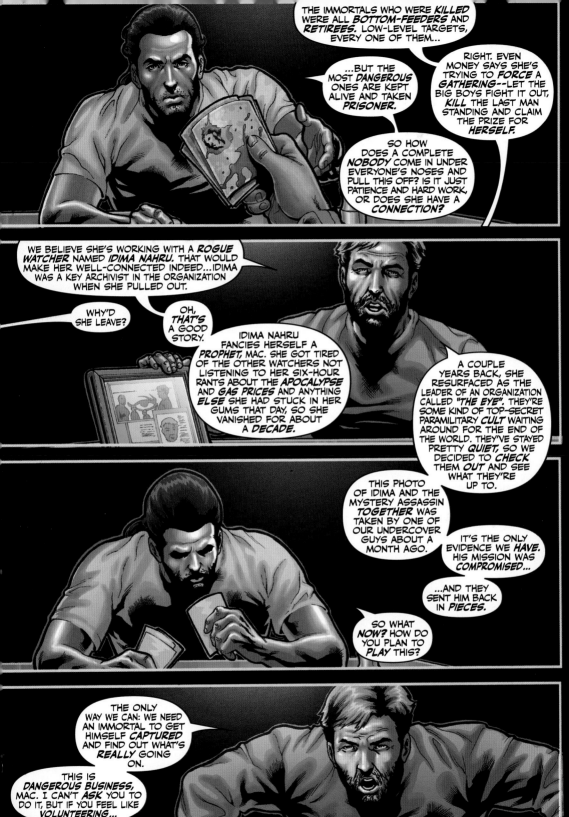

THE IMMORTALS WHO WERE *KILLED* WERE ALL *BOTTOM-FEEDERS* AND *RETIREES.* LOW-LEVEL TARGETS, EVERY ONE OF THEM...

...BUT THE MOST *DANGEROUS* ONES ARE KEPT ALIVE AND TAKEN *PRISONER.*

RIGHT. EVEN MONEY SAYS SHE'S TRYING TO *FORCE* A *GATHERING*--LET THE BIG BOYS FIGHT IT OUT, *KILL* THE LAST MAN STANDING AND CLAIM THE PRIZE FOR *HERSELF.*

SO HOW DOES A COMPLETE *NOBODY* COME IN UNDER EVERYONE'S NOSES AND PULL THIS OFF? IS IT JUST PATIENCE AND HARD WORK, OR DOES SHE HAVE A *CONNECTION?*

WE BELIEVE SHE'S WORKING WITH A *ROGUE WATCHER* NAMED *IDIMA NAHRU.* THAT WOULD MAKE HER WELL-CONNECTED INDEED...IDIMA WAS A KEY ARCHIVIST IN THE ORGANIZATION WHEN SHE PULLED OUT.

WHY'D SHE LEAVE?

OH, *THAT'S* A GOOD STORY.

IDIMA NAHRU FANCIES HERSELF A *PROPHET,* MAC. SHE GOT TIRED OF THE OTHER WATCHERS NOT LISTENING TO HER SIX-HOUR RANTS ABOUT THE *APOCALYPSE* AND *GAS PRICES* AND ANYTHING *ELSE* SHE HAD STUCK IN HER GUMS THAT DAY, SO SHE VANISHED FOR ABOUT A *DECADE.*

A COUPLE YEARS BACK, SHE RESURFACED AS THE LEADER OF AN ORGANIZATION CALLED *"THE EYE".* THEY'RE SOME KIND OF TOP-SECRET PARAMILITARY *CULT* WAITING AROUND FOR THE END OF THE WORLD. THEY'VE STAYED PRETTY *QUIET,* SO WE DECIDED TO *CHECK* THEM *OUT* AND SEE WHAT THEY'RE UP TO.

THIS PHOTO OF IDIMA AND THE MYSTERY ASSASSIN *TOGETHER* WAS TAKEN BY ONE OF OUR UNDERCOVER GUYS ABOUT A MONTH AGO.

IT'S THE ONLY EVIDENCE WE *HAVE.* HIS MISSION WAS *COMPROMISED...*

...AND THEY SENT HIM BACK IN *PIECES.*

SO WHAT *NOW?* HOW DO YOU PLAN TO *PLAY* THIS?

THE ONLY WAY WE CAN: WE NEED AN IMMORTAL TO GET HIMSELF *CAPTURED* AND FIND OUT WHAT'S *REALLY* GOING ON.

THIS IS *DANGEROUS BUSINESS,* MAC. I CAN'T *ASK* YOU TO DO IT, BUT IF YOU FEEL LIKE *VOLUNTEERING...*

THINK IT OVER. I'LL BE IN THE HALL.

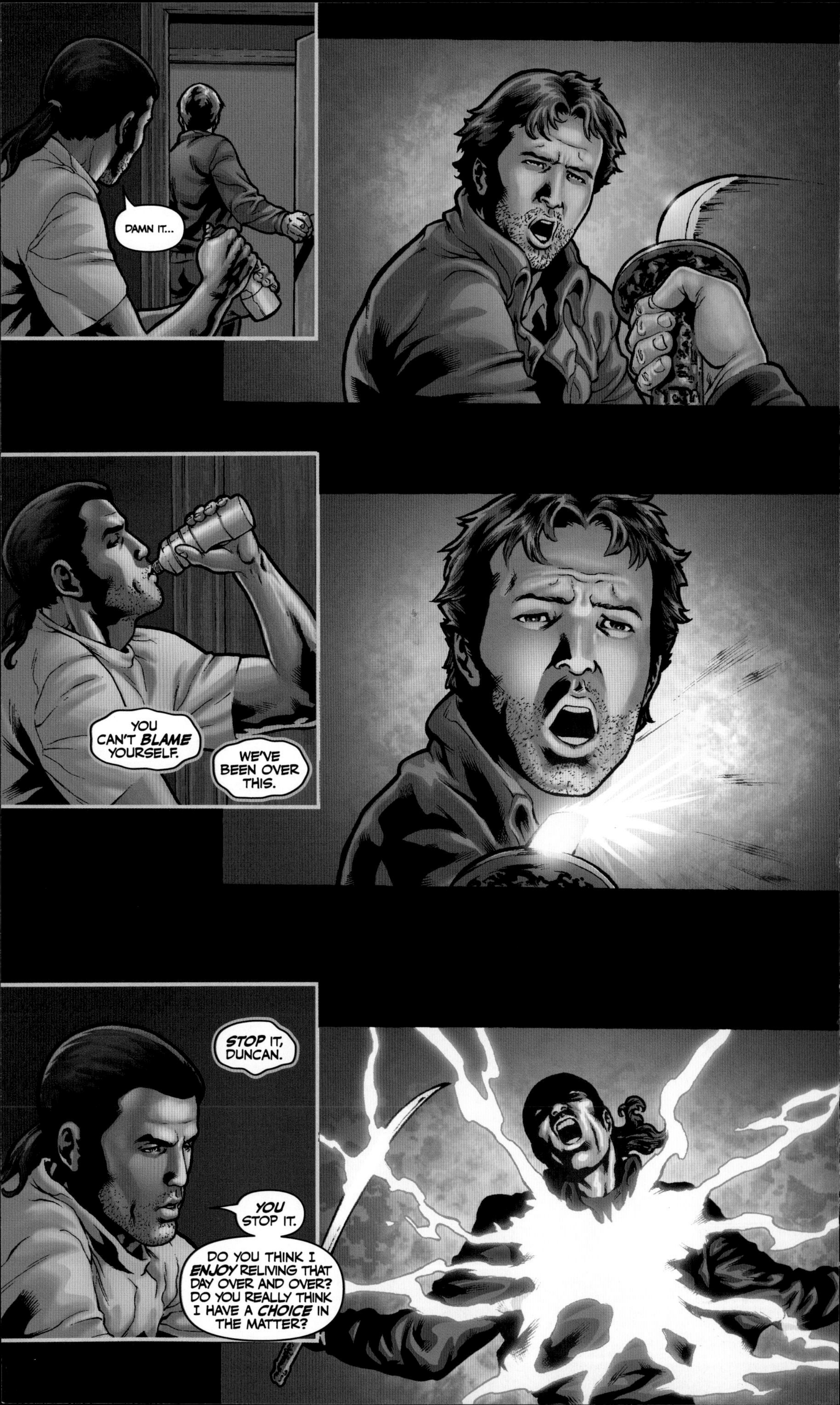
DAMN IT...
YOU CAN'T BLAME YOURSELF.
WE'VE BEEN OVER THIS.
STOP IT, DUNCAN.
YOU STOP IT.
DO YOU THINK I ENJOY RELIVING THAT DAY OVER AND OVER? DO YOU REALLY THINK I HAVE A CHOICE IN THE MATTER?

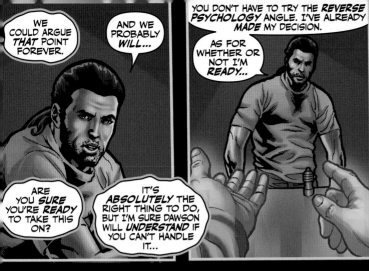

WE COULD ARGUE *THAT* POINT FOREVER.

AND WE PROBABLY *WILL*...

ARE YOU *SURE* YOU'RE *READY* TO TAKE THIS ON?

IT'S *ABSOLUTELY* THE RIGHT THING TO DO, BUT I'M SURE DAWSON WILL *UNDERSTAND* IF YOU CAN'T HANDLE IT...

YOU DON'T HAVE TO TRY THE *REVERSE PSYCHOLOGY* ANGLE. I'VE ALREADY *MADE* MY DECISION.

AS FOR WHETHER OR NOT I'M *READY*...

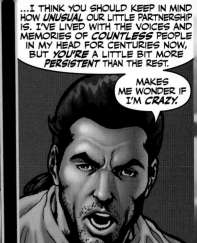

...I THINK YOU SHOULD KEEP IN MIND HOW *UNUSUAL* OUR LITTLE PARTNERSHIP IS. I'VE LIVED WITH THE VOICES AND MEMORIES OF *COUNTLESS* PEOPLE IN MY HEAD FOR CENTURIES NOW, BUT *YOU'RE* A LITTLE BIT MORE *PERSISTENT* THAN THE REST.

MAKES ME WONDER IF I'M *CRAZY*.

LOOK AT IT *THIS* WAY, COUSIN...

...IF *YOU'RE* CRAZY, WHAT DOES THAT MAKE ME?

MAC...?

I'VE MADE UP MY *MIND*, JOE.

I'M GOING *IN*.

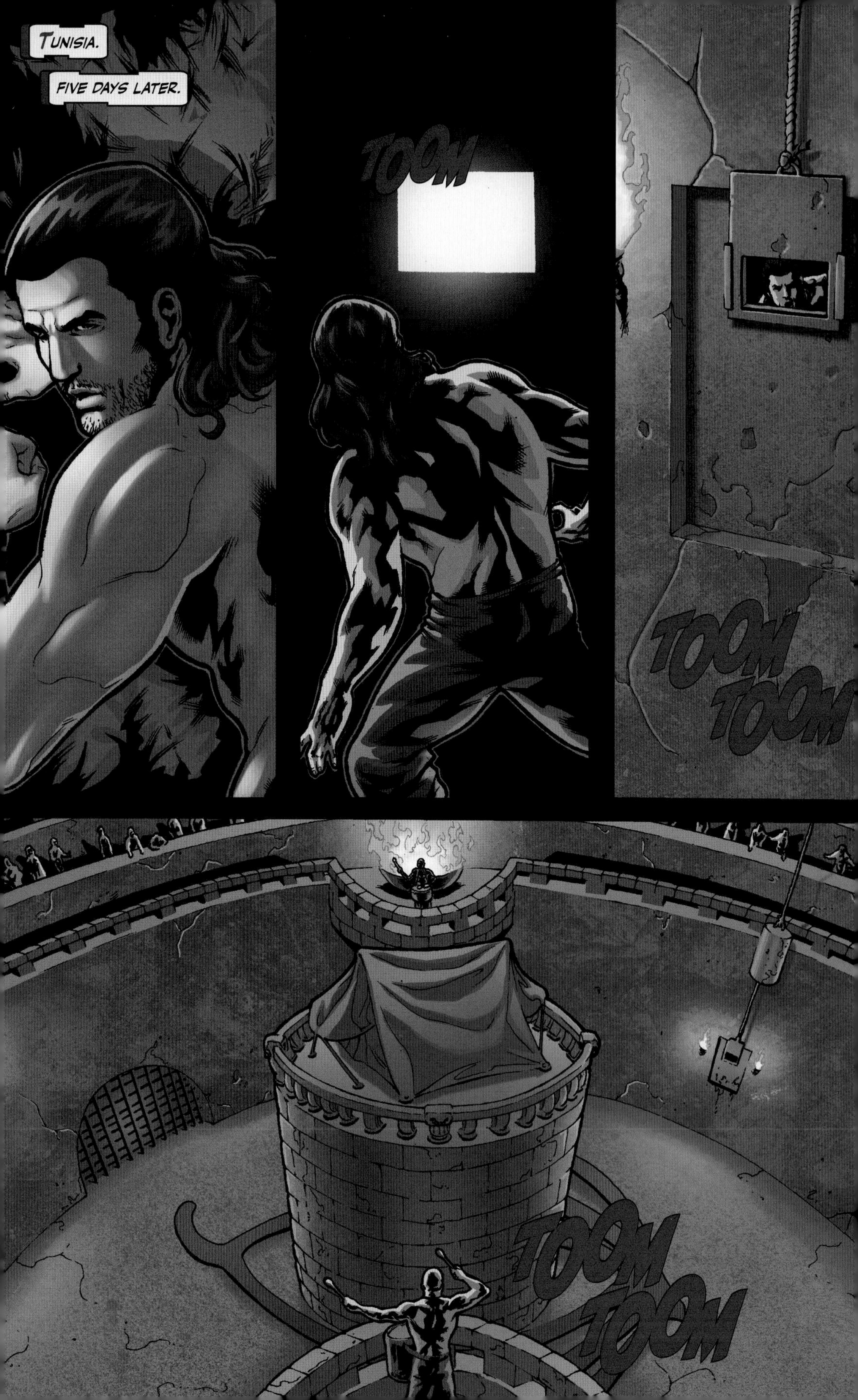
Tunisia.
Five days later.
TOOM
TOOM TOOM
TOOM TOOM

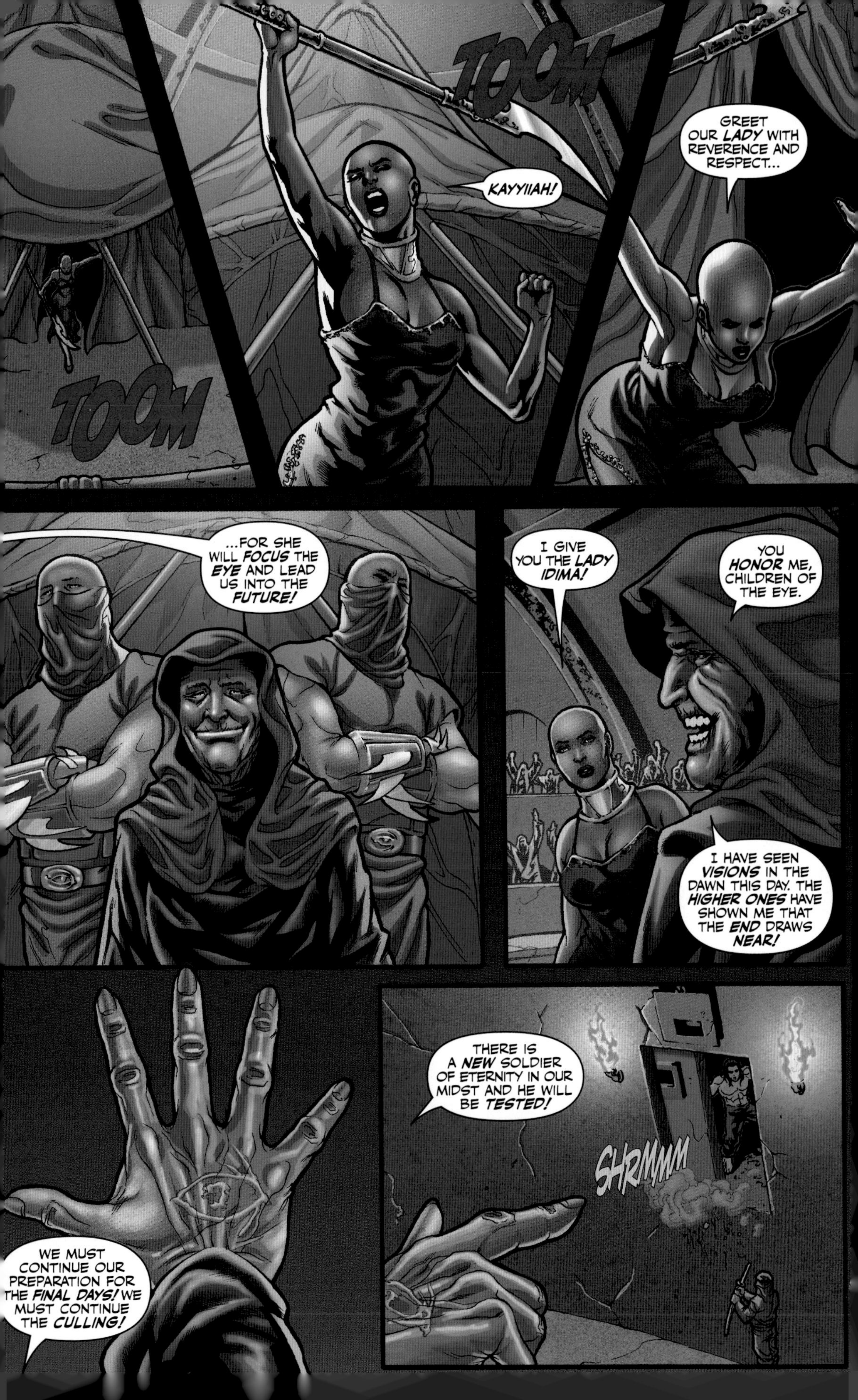
TOOM
KAYYIIAH!
TOOM
GREET OUR LADY WITH REVERENCE AND RESPECT...
...FOR SHE WILL FOCUS THE EYE AND LEAD US INTO THE FUTURE!
I GIVE YOU THE LADY IDIMA!
YOU HONOR ME, CHILDREN OF THE EYE.
I HAVE SEEN VISIONS IN THE DAWN THIS DAY. THE HIGHER ONES HAVE SHOWN ME THAT THE END DRAWS NEAR!
WE MUST CONTINUE OUR PREPARATION FOR THE FINAL DAYS! WE MUST CONTINUE THE CULLING!
THERE IS A NEW SOLDIER OF ETERNITY IN OUR MIDST AND HE WILL BE TESTED!
SHRMMM

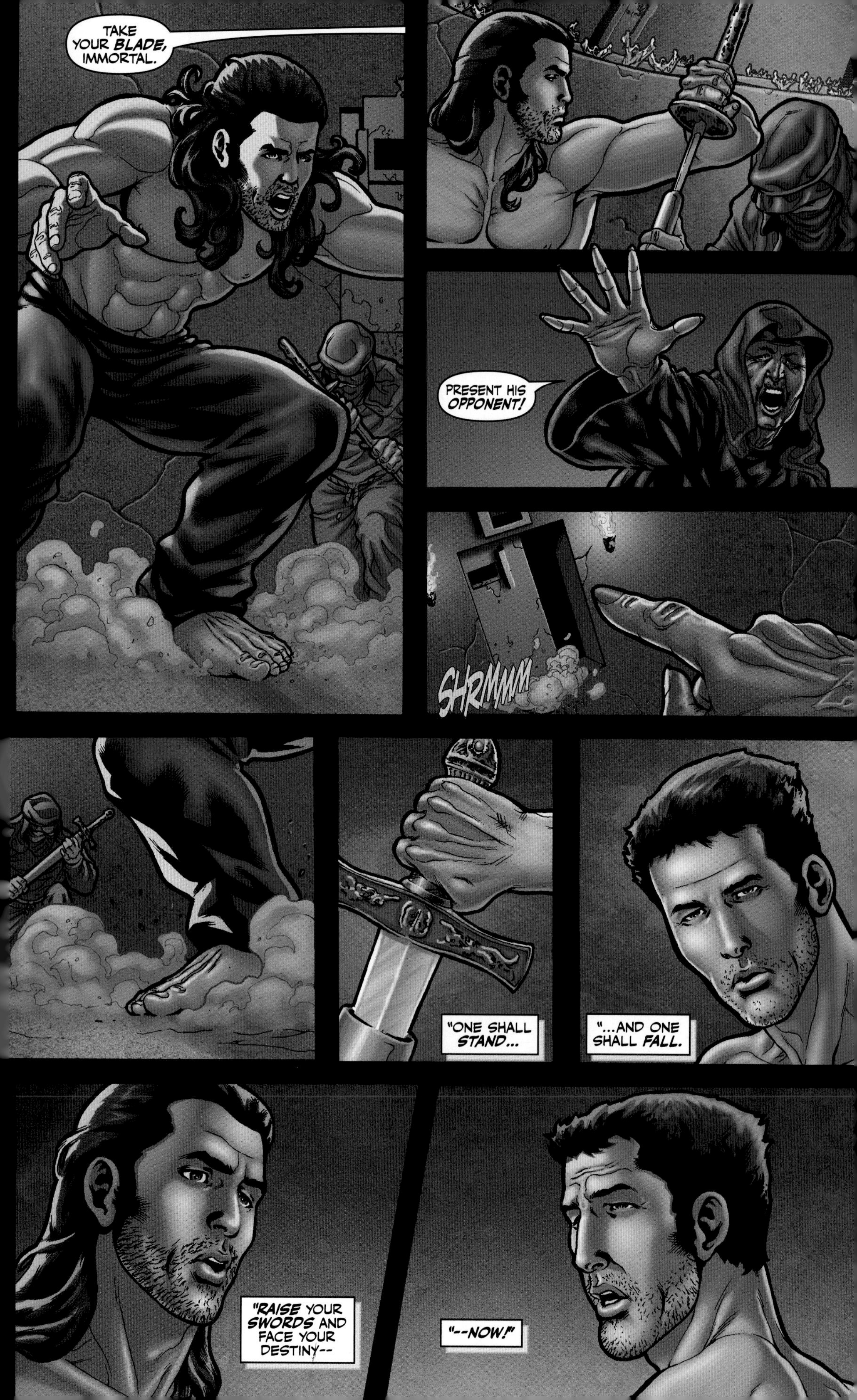
TAKE YOUR BLADE, IMMORTAL.
PRESENT HIS OPPONENT!
SHRMMM
"ONE SHALL STAND...
"...AND ONE SHALL FALL.
"RAISE YOUR SWORDS AND FACE YOUR DESTINY--
"--NOW!"

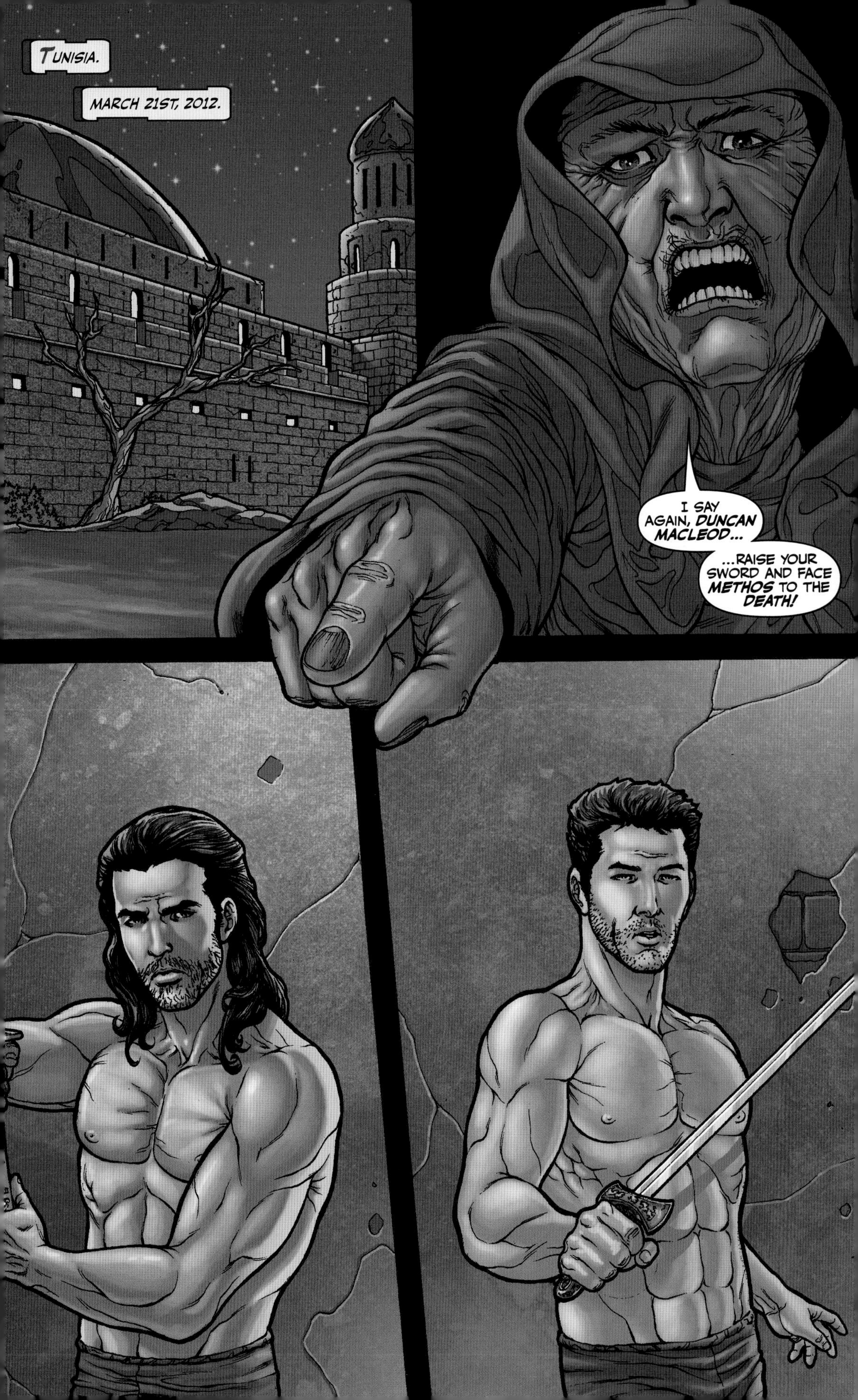
TUNISIA.
MARCH 21ST, 2012.
I SAY AGAIN, DUNCAN MACLEOD...
...RAISE YOUR SWORD AND FACE METHOS TO THE DEATH!

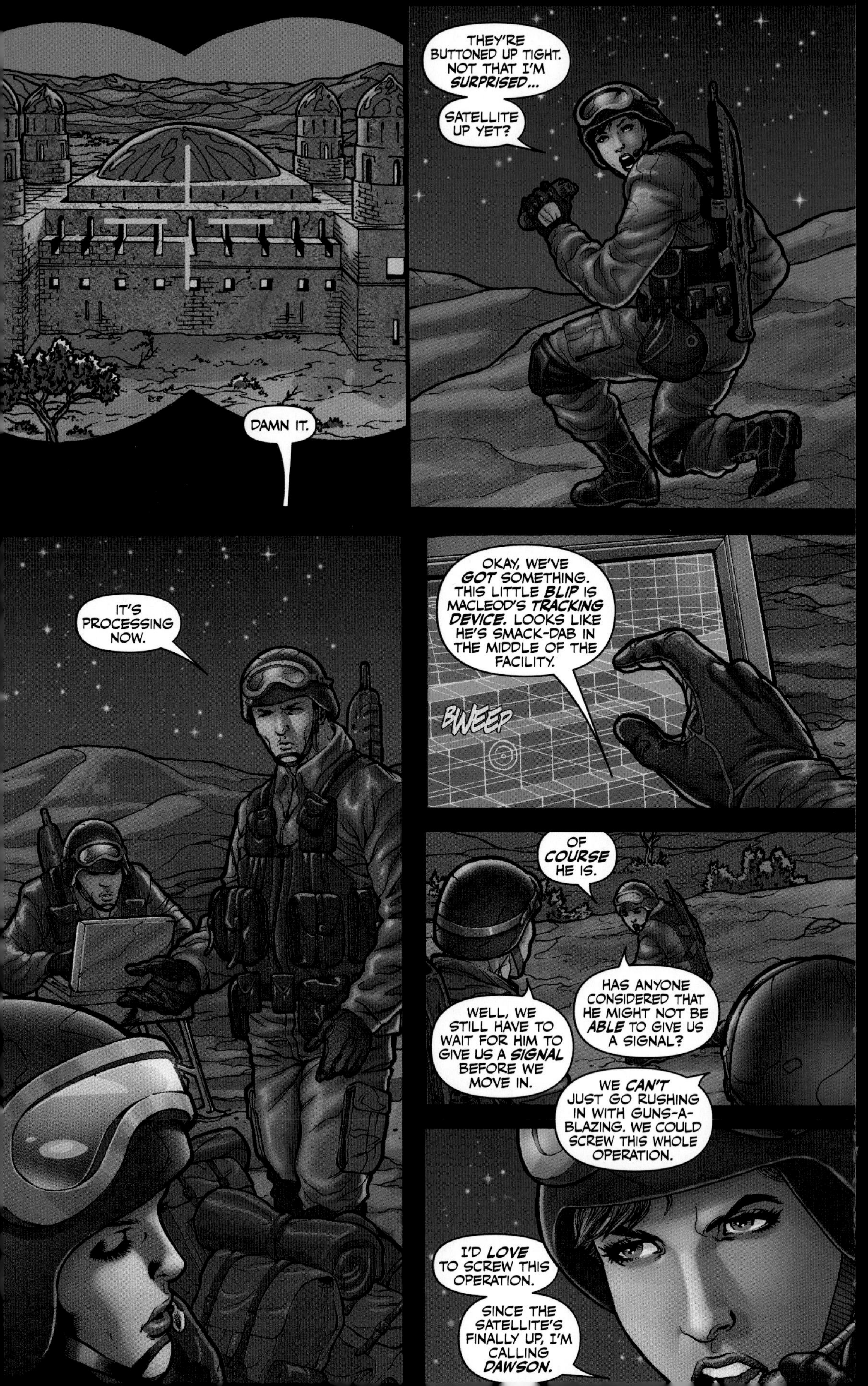
DAMN IT.
THEY'RE BUTTONED UP TIGHT. NOT THAT I'M SURPRISED...
SATELLITE UP YET?
IT'S PROCESSING NOW.
OKAY, WE'VE GOT SOMETHING. THIS LITTLE BLIP IS MACLEOD'S TRACKING DEVICE. LOOKS LIKE HE'S SMACK-DAB IN THE MIDDLE OF THE FACILITY.
BWEEP
OF COURSE HE IS.
WELL, WE STILL HAVE TO WAIT FOR HIM TO GIVE US A SIGNAL BEFORE WE MOVE IN.
HAS ANYONE CONSIDERED THAT HE MIGHT NOT BE ABLE TO GIVE US A SIGNAL?
WE CAN'T JUST GO RUSHING IN WITH GUNS-A-BLAZING. WE COULD SCREW THIS WHOLE OPERATION.
I'D LOVE TO SCREW THIS OPERATION.
SINCE THE SATELLITE'S FINALLY UP, I'M CALLING DAWSON.

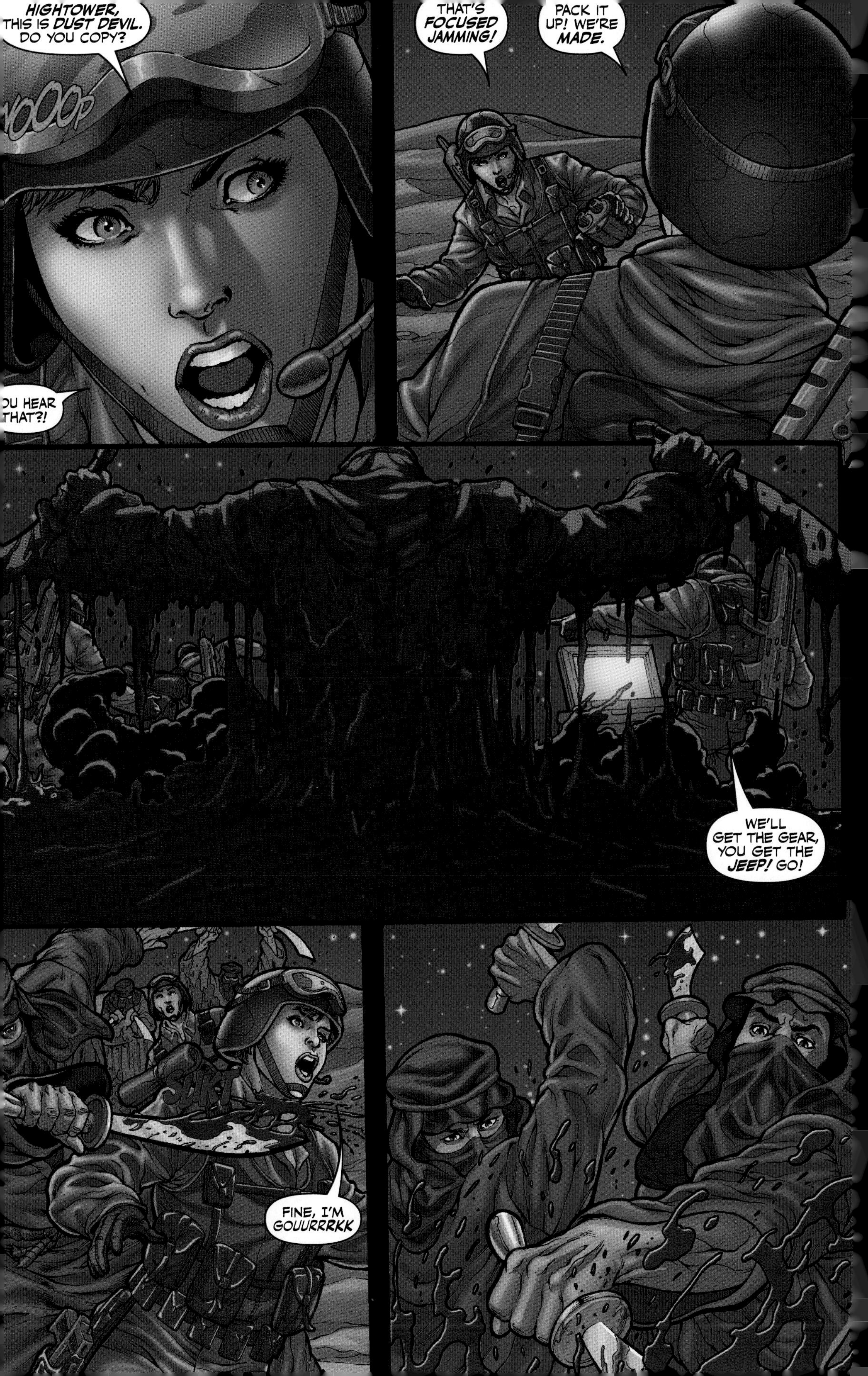
HIGHTOWER, THIS IS DUST DEVIL. DO YOU COPY?
OU HEAR THAT?!
THAT'S FOCUSED JAMMING!
PACK IT UP! WE'RE MADE.
WE'LL GET THE GEAR, YOU GET THE JEEP! GO!
FINE, I'M GOUURRRKK

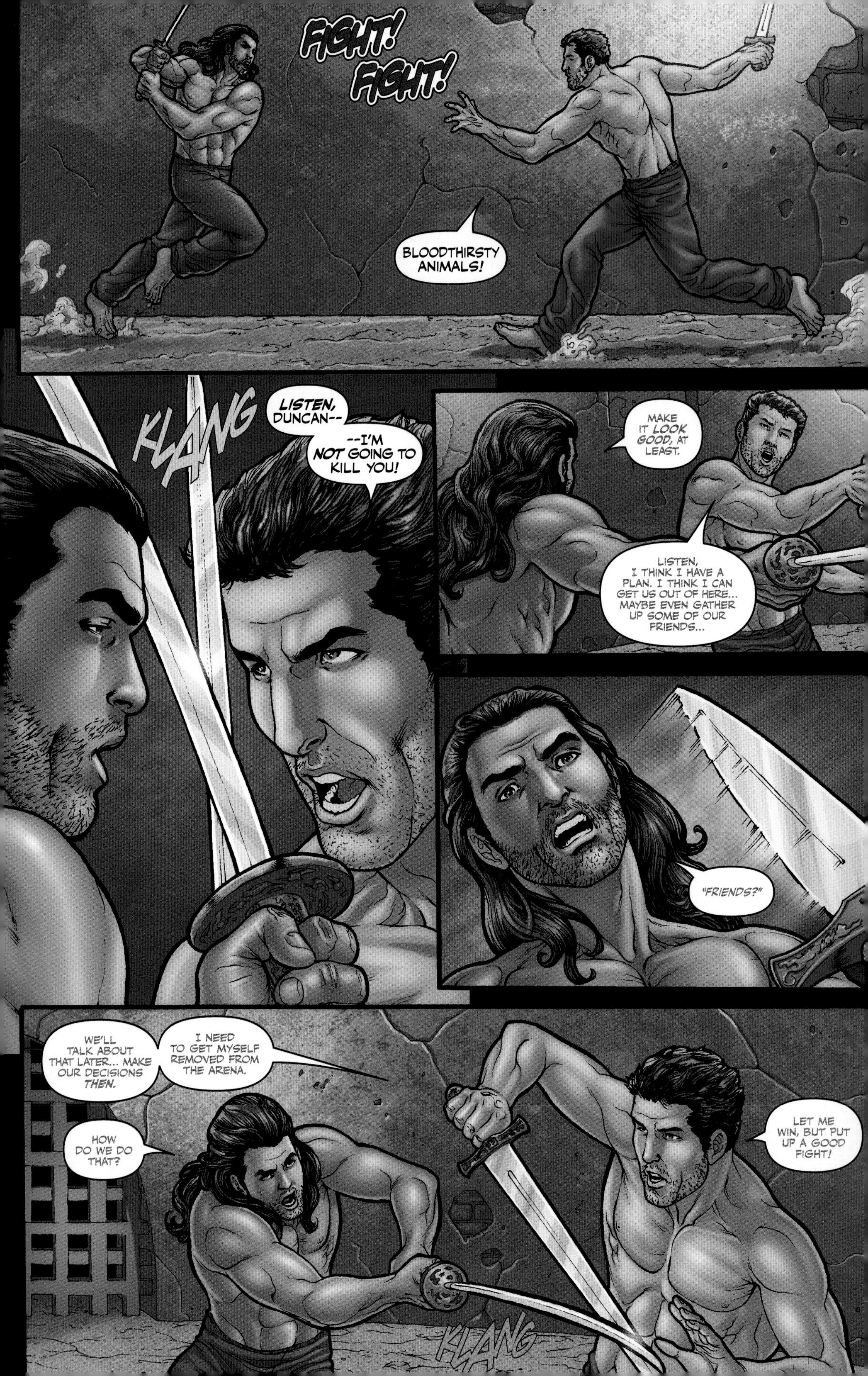
FIGHT! FIGHT!
BLOODTHIRSTY ANIMALS!
KLANG
LISTEN, DUNCAN--
--I'M NOT GOING TO KILL YOU!
MAKE IT LOOK GOOD, AT LEAST.
LISTEN, I THINK I HAVE A PLAN. I THINK I CAN GET US OUT OF HERE... MAYBE EVEN GATHER UP SOME OF OUR FRIENDS...
"FRIENDS?"
WE'LL TALK ABOUT THAT LATER... MAKE OUR DECISIONS THEN.
I NEED TO GET MYSELF REMOVED FROM THE ARENA.
HOW DO WE DO THAT?
LET ME WIN, BUT PUT UP A GOOD FIGHT!
KLANG

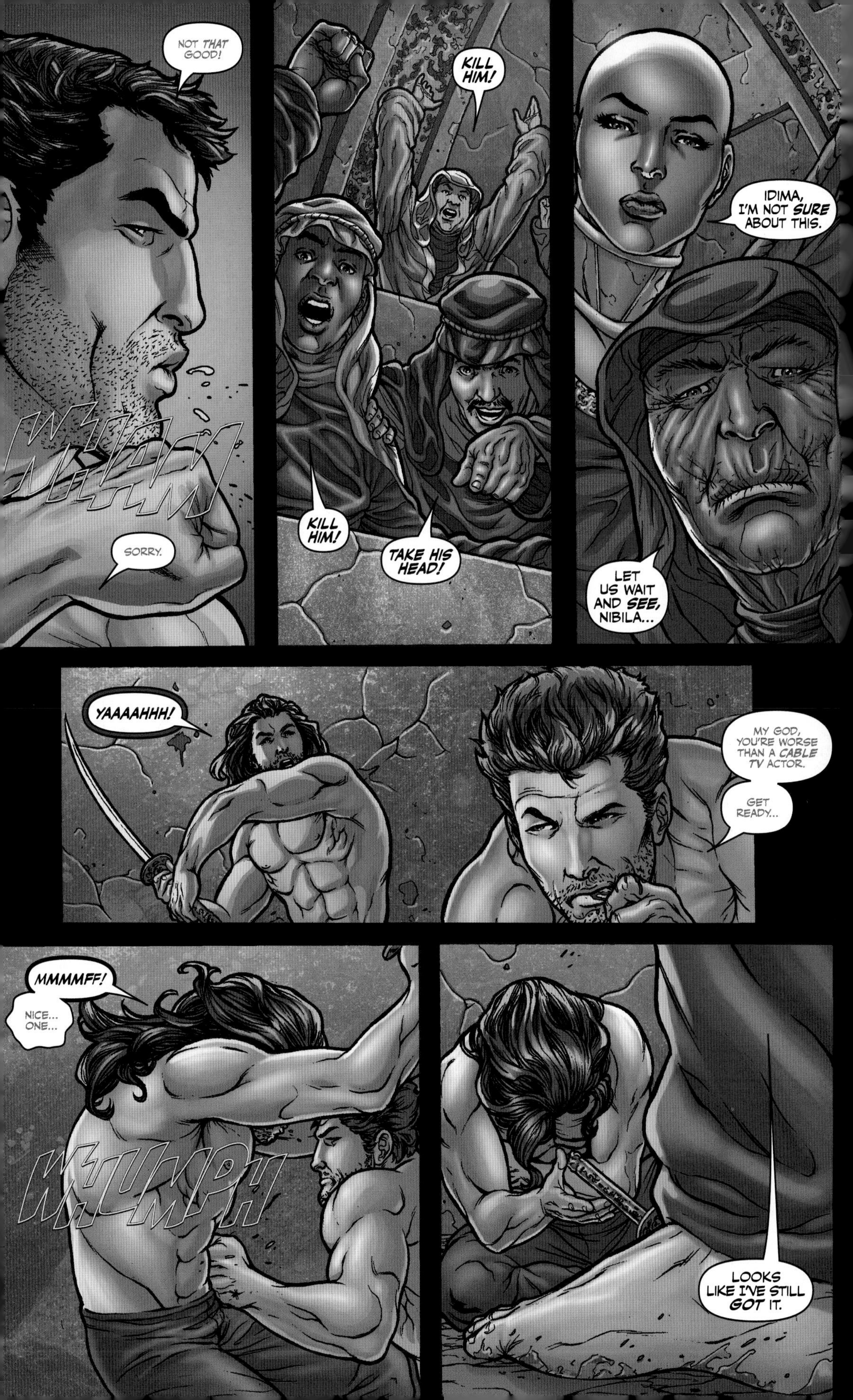
NOT THAT GOOD!
WHAM
SORRY.
KILL HIM!
KILL HIM!
TAKE HIS HEAD!
IDIMA, I'M NOT SURE ABOUT THIS.
LET US WAIT AND SEE, NIBILA...
YAAAAHHH!
MY GOD, YOU'RE WORSE THAN A CABLE TV ACTOR.
GET READY...
MMMMFF!
NICE... ONE...
WHUMPH
LOOKS LIKE I'VE STILL GOT IT.

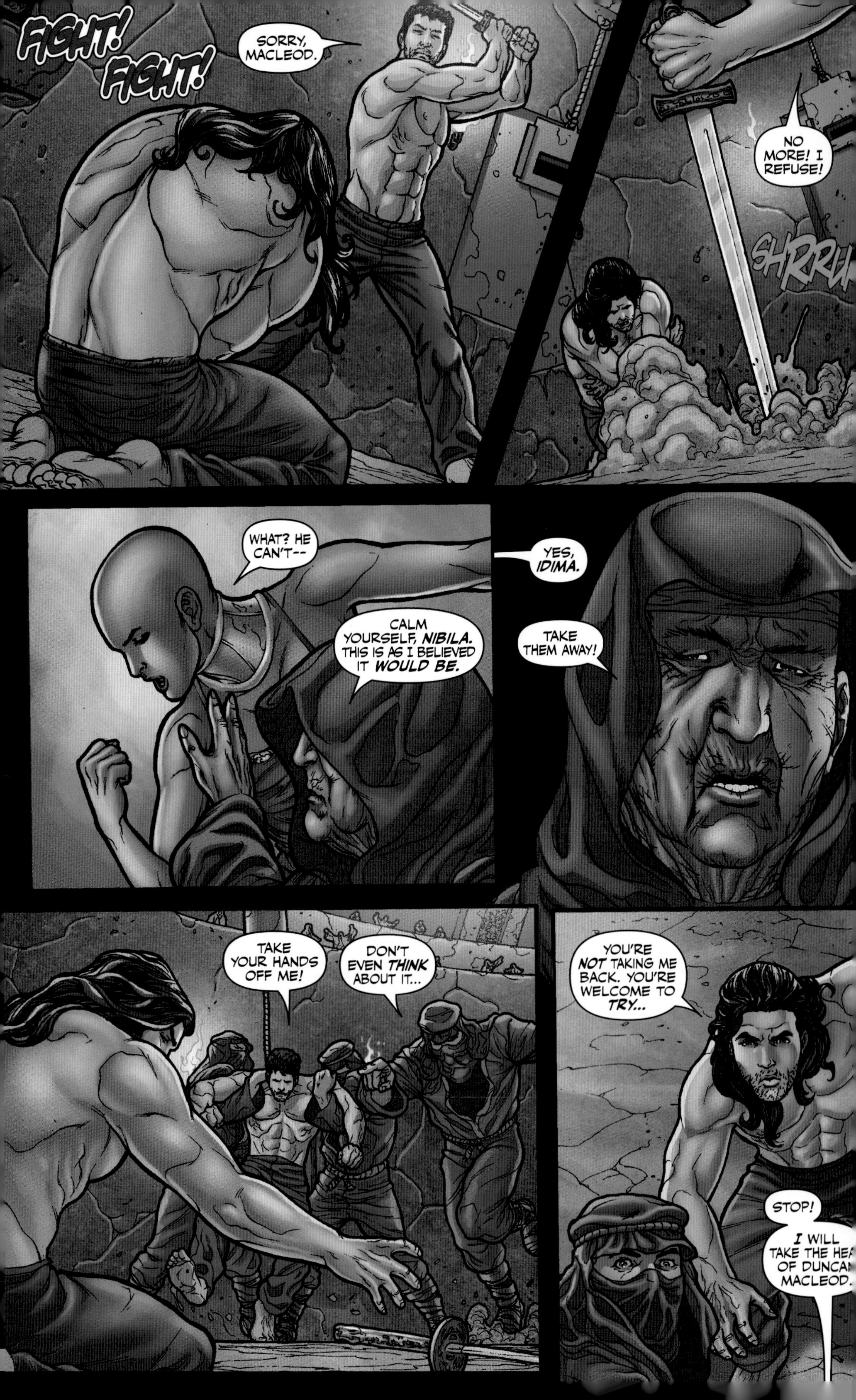
FIGHT! FIGHT!
SORRY, MACLEOD.
NO MORE! I REFUSE!
SHRRU
WHAT? HE CAN'T--
CALM YOURSELF, NIBILA. THIS IS AS I BELIEVED IT WOULD BE.
YES, IDIMA.
TAKE THEM AWAY!
TAKE YOUR HANDS OFF ME!
DON'T EVEN THINK ABOUT IT...
YOU'RE NOT TAKING ME BACK. YOU'RE WELCOME TO TRY...
STOP!
I WILL TAKE THE HEA OF DUNCAN MACLEOD.

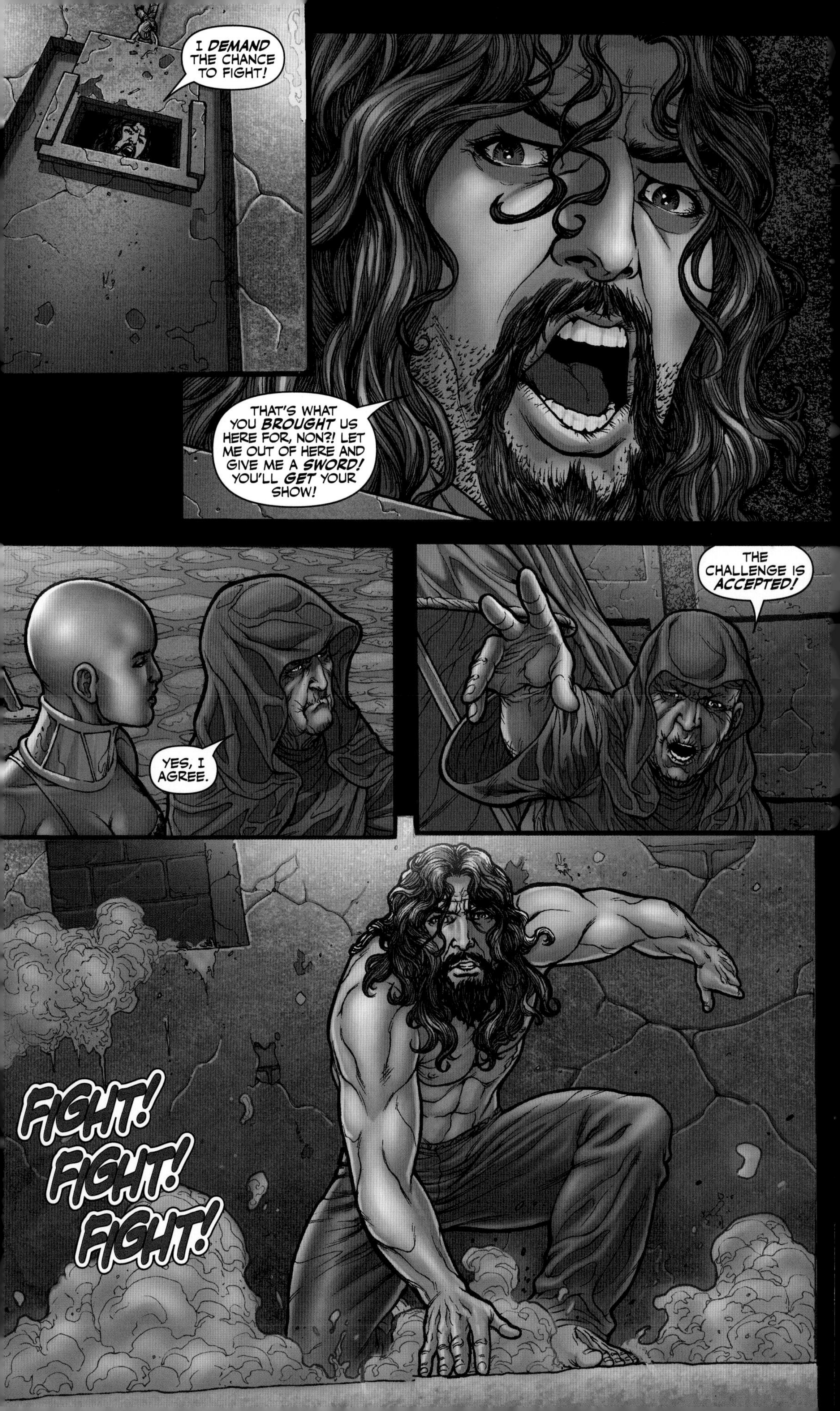
I DEMAND THE CHANCE TO FIGHT!
THAT'S WHAT YOU BROUGHT US HERE FOR, NON?! LET ME OUT OF HERE AND GIVE ME A SWORD! YOU'LL GET YOUR SHOW!
YES, I AGREE.
THE CHALLENGE IS ACCEPTED!
FIGHT! FIGHT! FIGHT!

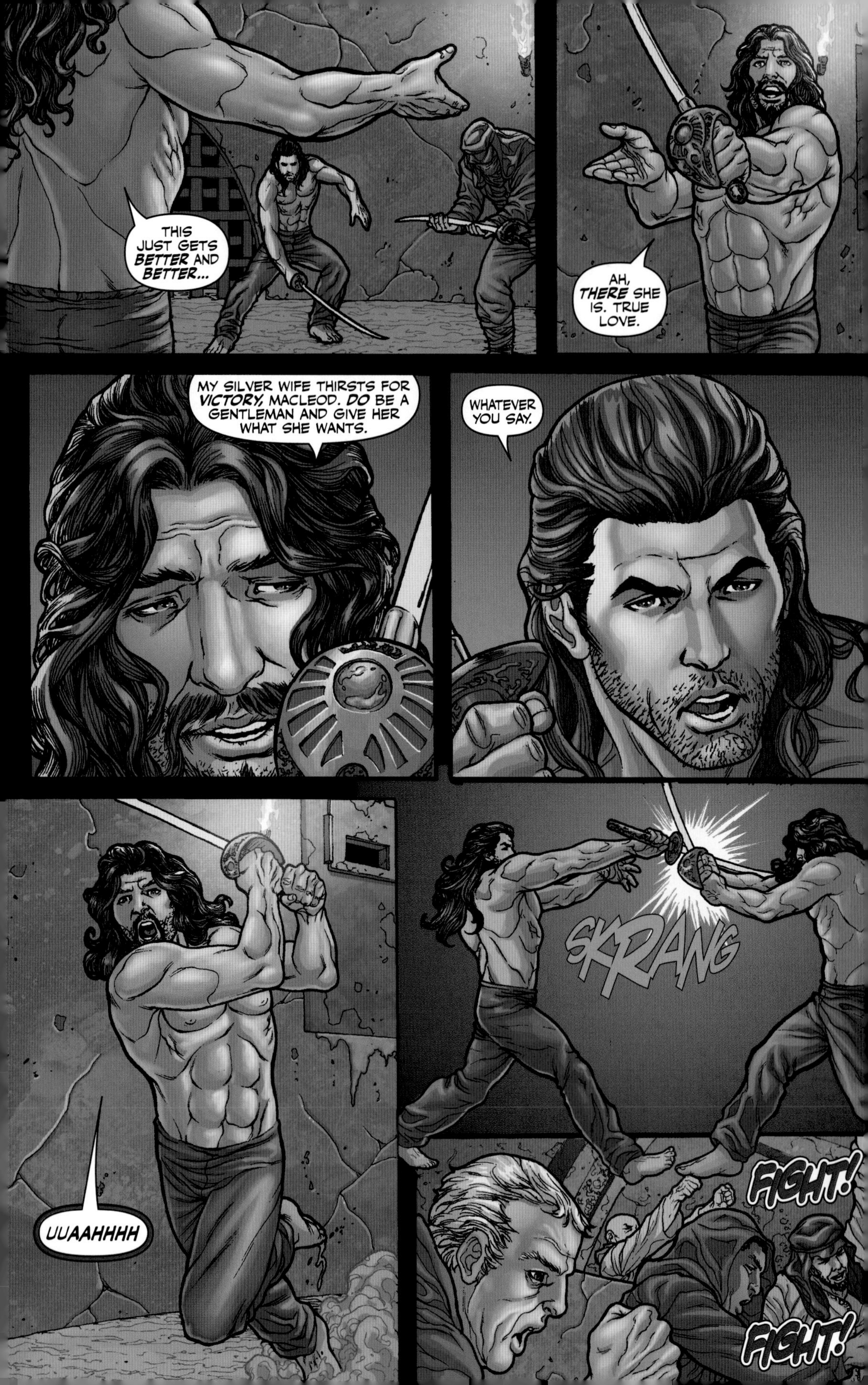
THIS JUST GETS BETTER AND BETTER...
AH, THERE SHE IS. TRUE LOVE.
MY SILVER WIFE THIRSTS FOR VICTORY, MACLEOD. DO BE A GENTLEMAN AND GIVE HER WHAT SHE WANTS.
WHATEVER YOU SAY.
UUAAHHHH
SKRANG
FIGHT!
FIGHT!

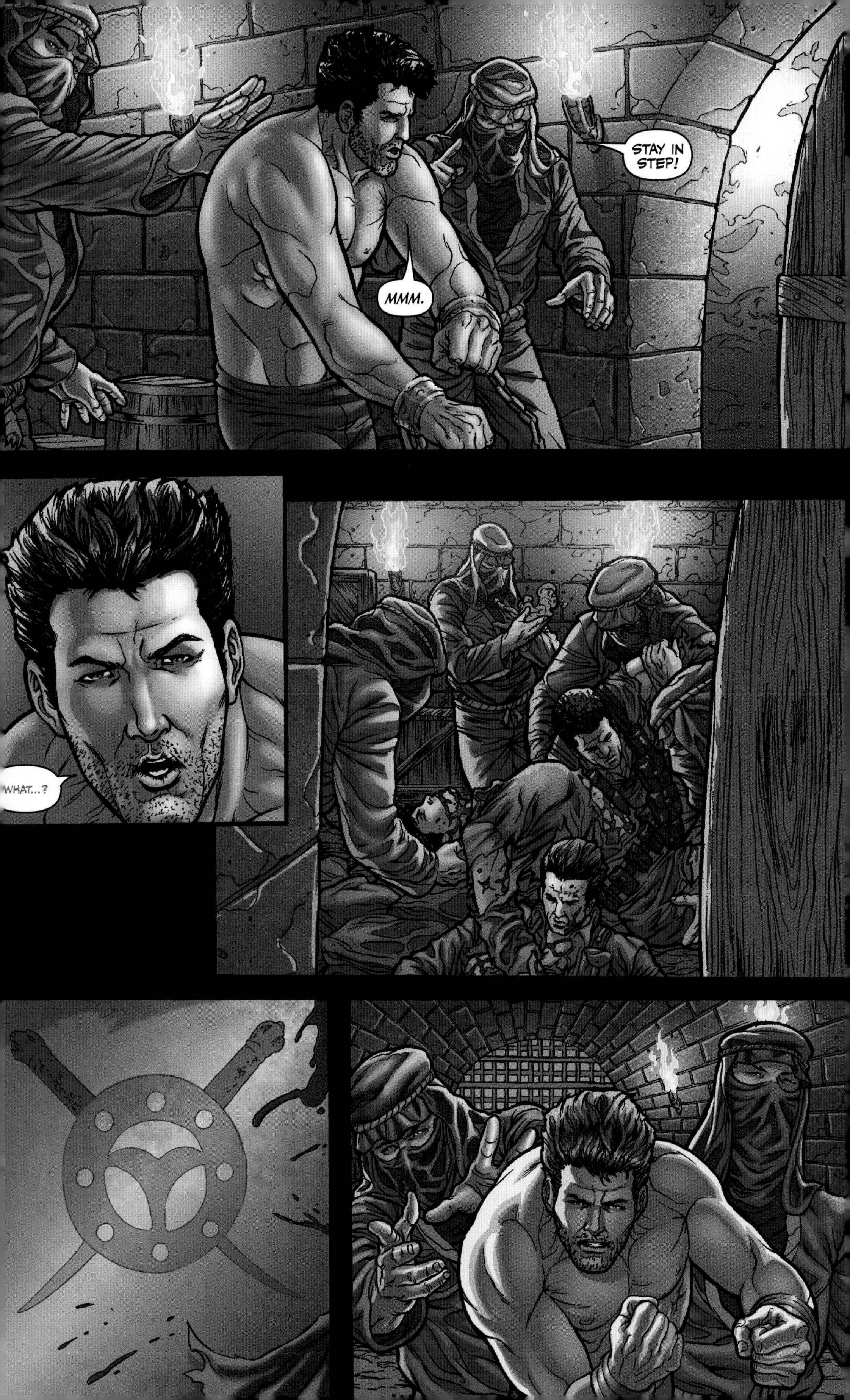
STAY IN STEP!
MMM.
WHAT...?

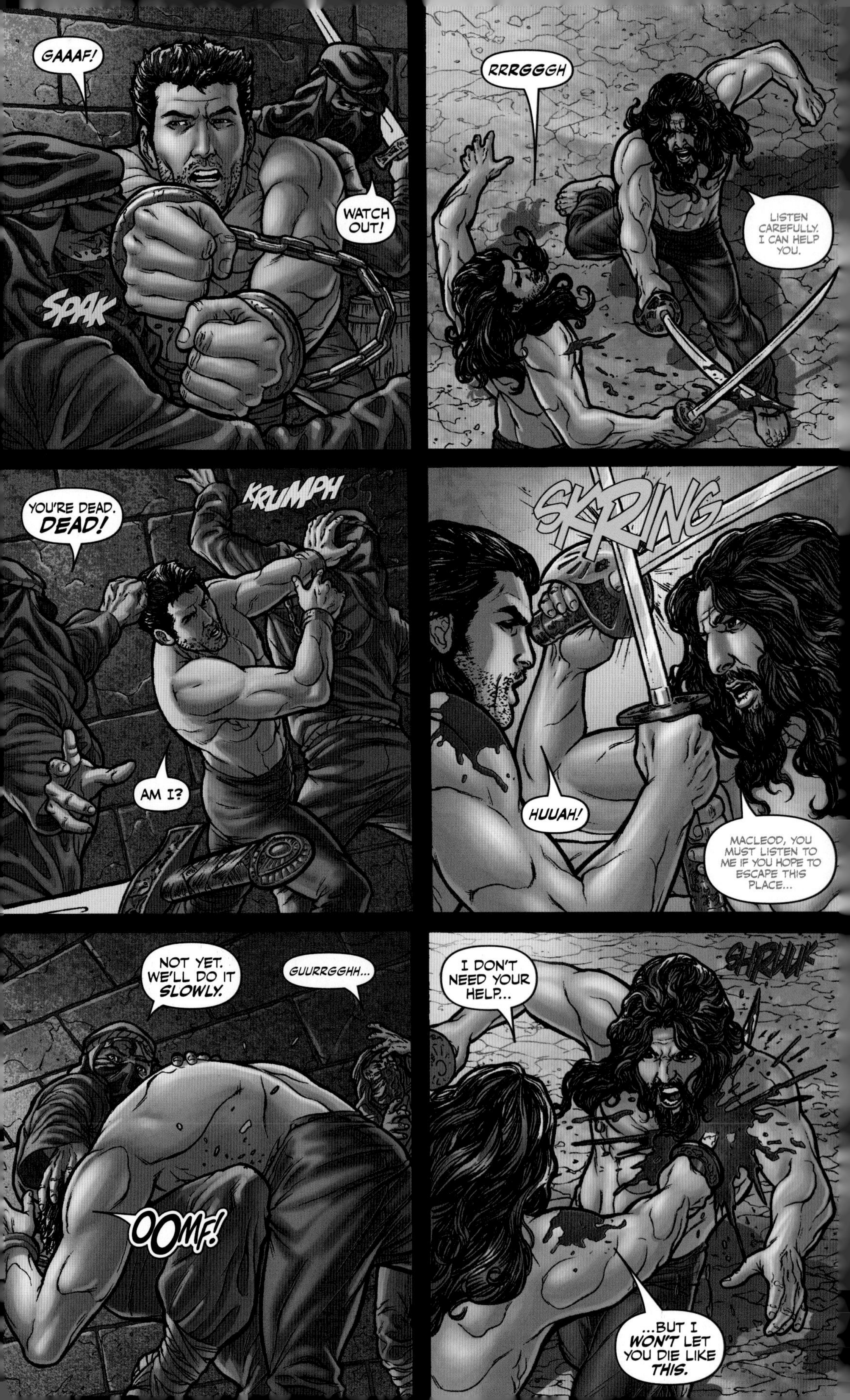
GAAAF!
WATCH OUT!
SPAK
RRRGGGH
LISTEN CAREFULLY. I CAN HELP YOU.
YOU'RE DEAD. DEAD!
K'RUMPH
AM I?
SKRING
HUUAH!
MACLEOD, YOU MUST LISTEN TO ME IF YOU HOPE TO ESCAPE THIS PLACE...
NOT YET. WE'LL DO IT SLOWLY.
GUURRGGHH...
OOMF!
SHRUUK
I DON'T NEED YOUR HELP...
...BUT I WON'T LET YOU DIE LIKE THIS.

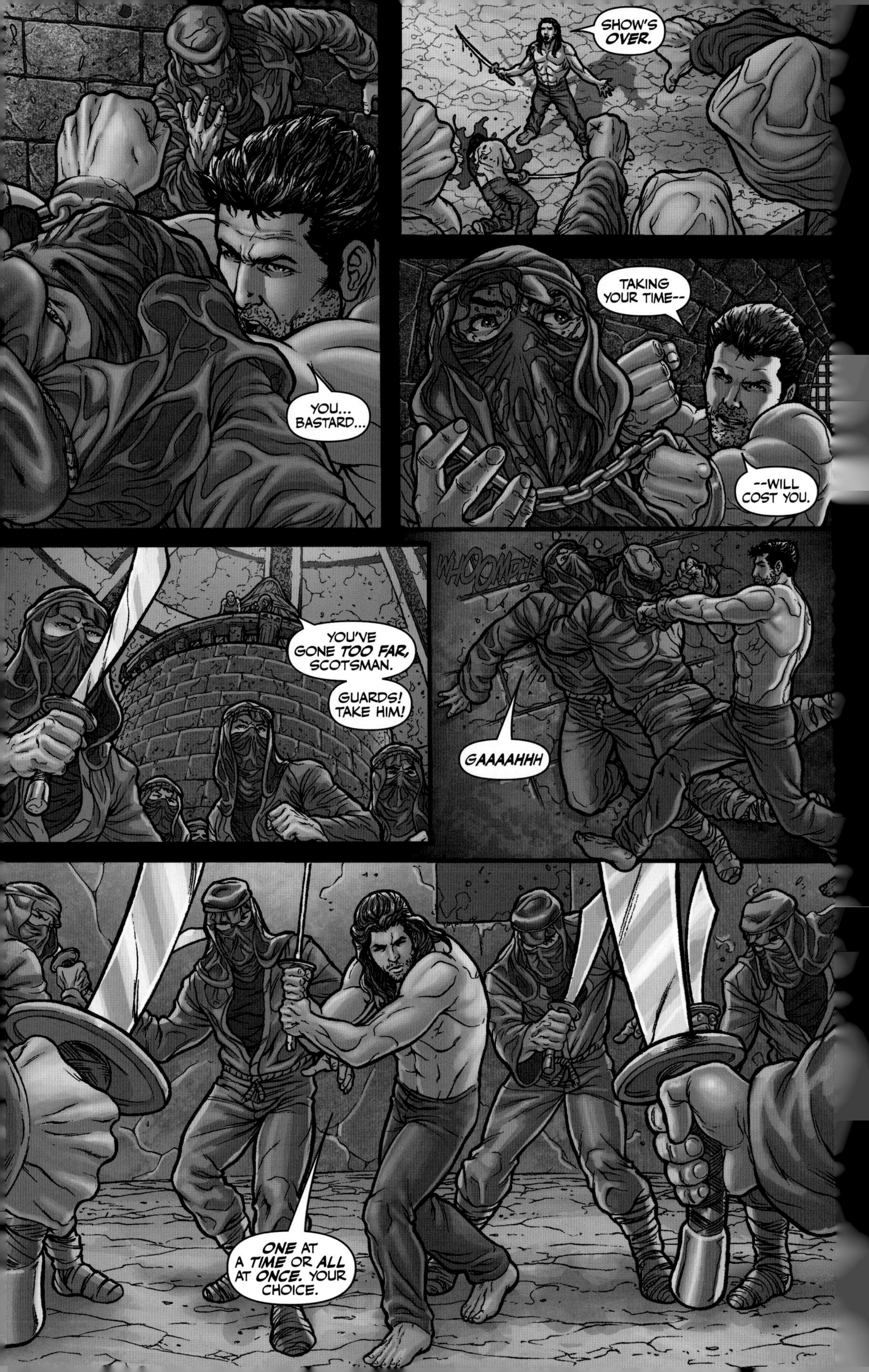
YOU... BASTARD...
SHOW'S *OVER.*
TAKING YOUR TIME--
--WILL COST YOU.
YOU'VE GONE *TOO FAR,* SCOTSMAN.
GUARDS! TAKE HIM!
WHOOMPH!
GAAAAHHH
ONE AT A *TIME* OR *ALL* AT *ONCE.* YOUR CHOICE.

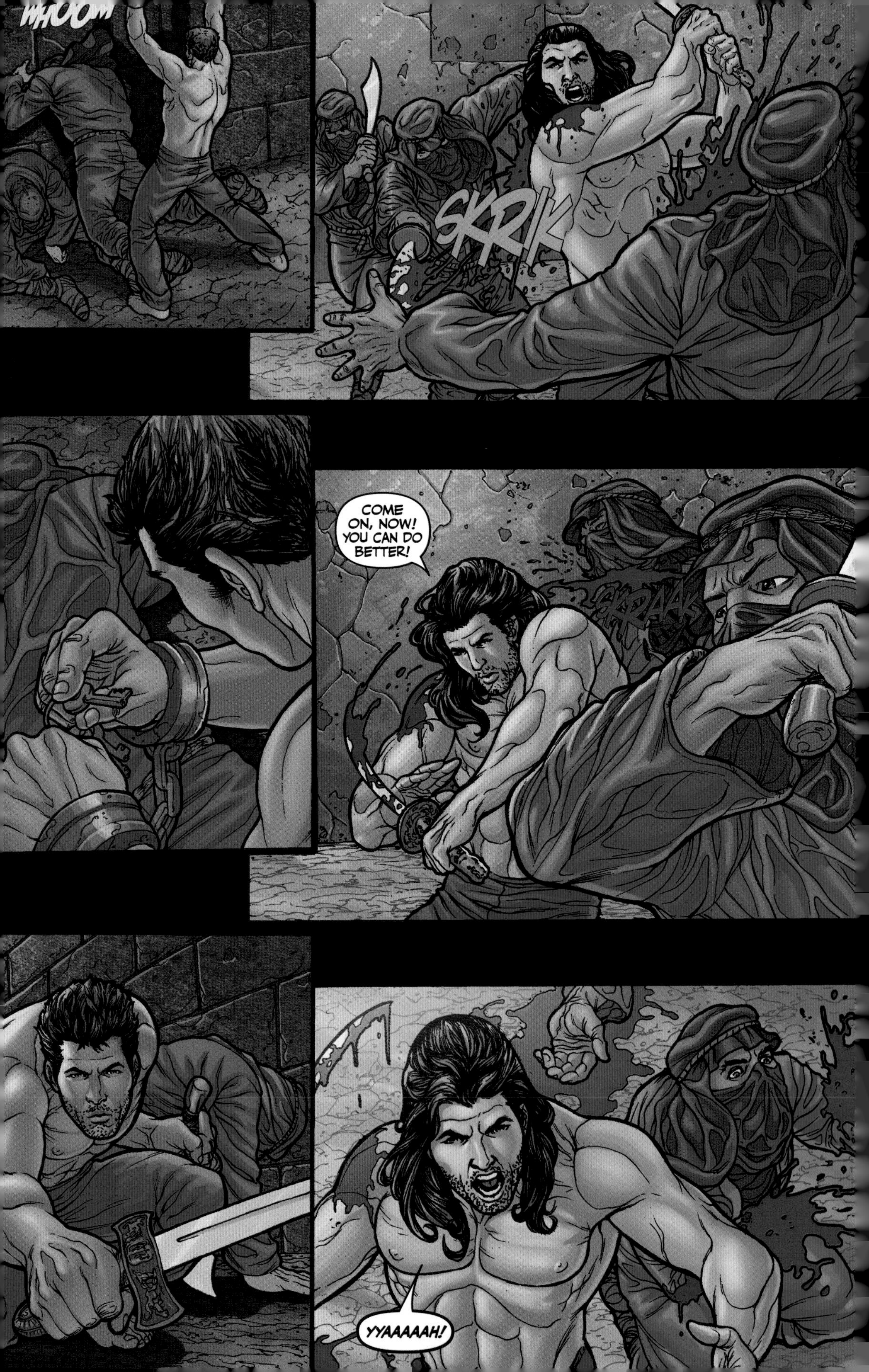
WHOOM
SKRIK
COME ON, NOW! YOU CAN DO BETTER!
SKRAAK
YYAAAAAH!

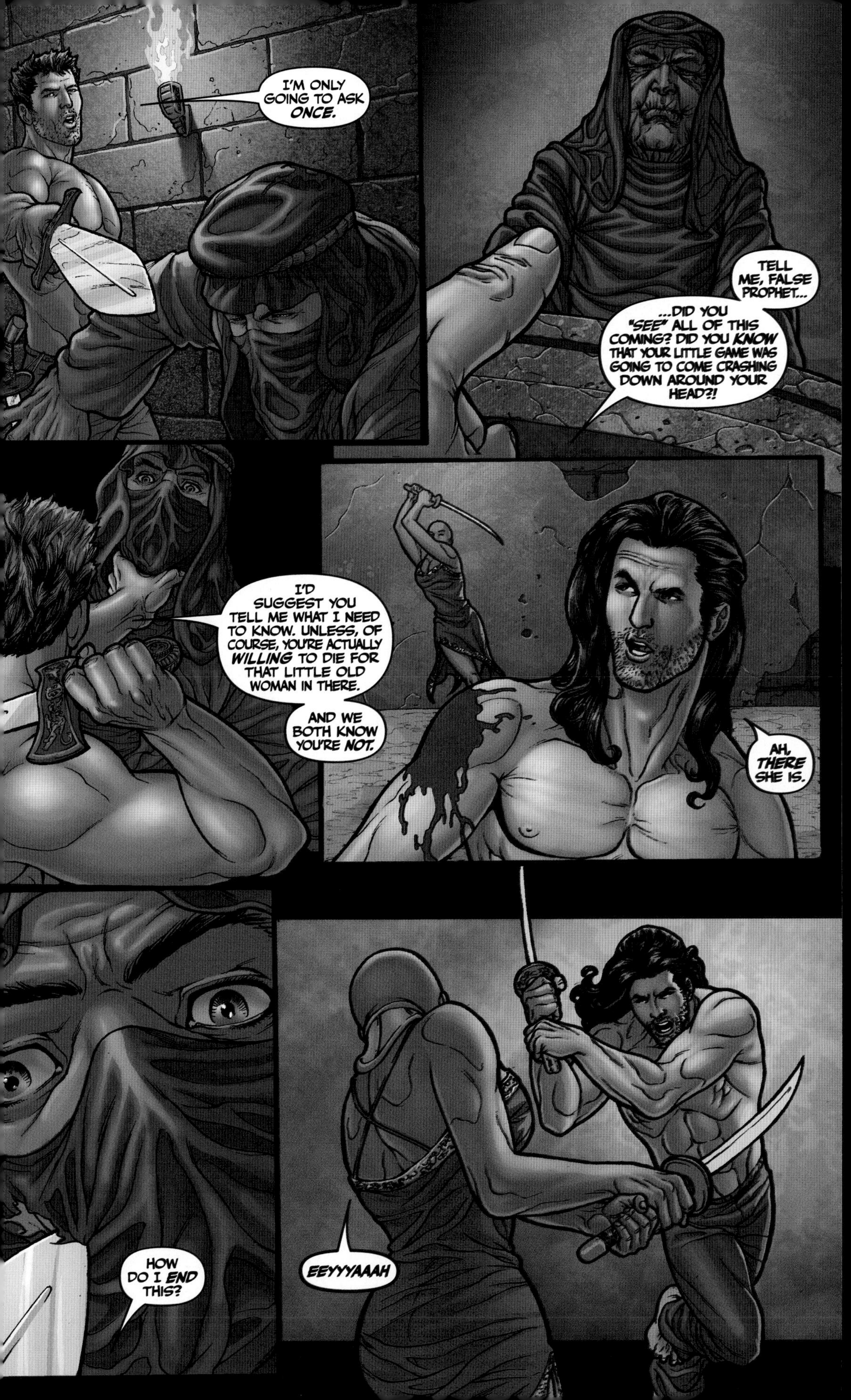
I'M ONLY GOING TO ASK ONCE.
TELL ME, FALSE PROPHET...
..."SEE" ALL OF THIS COMING? DID YOU KNOW THAT YOUR LITTLE GAME WAS GOING TO COME CRASHING DOWN AROUND YOUR HEAD?!
I'D SUGGEST YOU TELL ME WHAT I NEED TO KNOW. UNLESS, OF COURSE, YOU'RE ACTUALLY WILLING TO DIE FOR THAT LITTLE OLD WOMAN IN THERE.
AND WE BOTH KNOW YOU'RE NOT.
AH, THERE SHE IS.
HOW DO I END THIS?
EEYYYAAAH

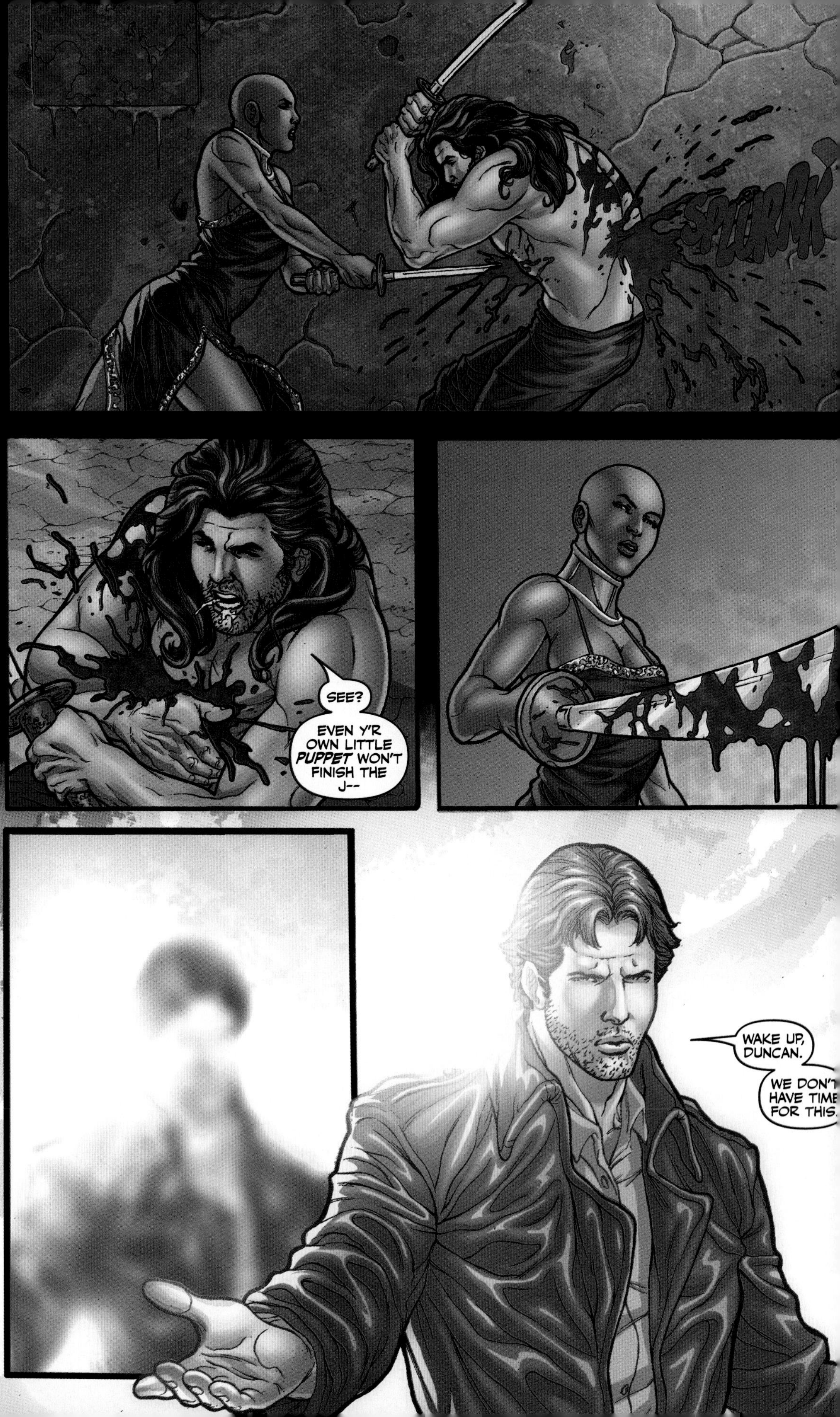
SPLURKK
SEE?
EVEN Y'R OWN LITTLE PUPPET WON'T FINISH THE J--
WAKE UP, DUNCAN.
WE DON'T HAVE TIME FOR THIS.

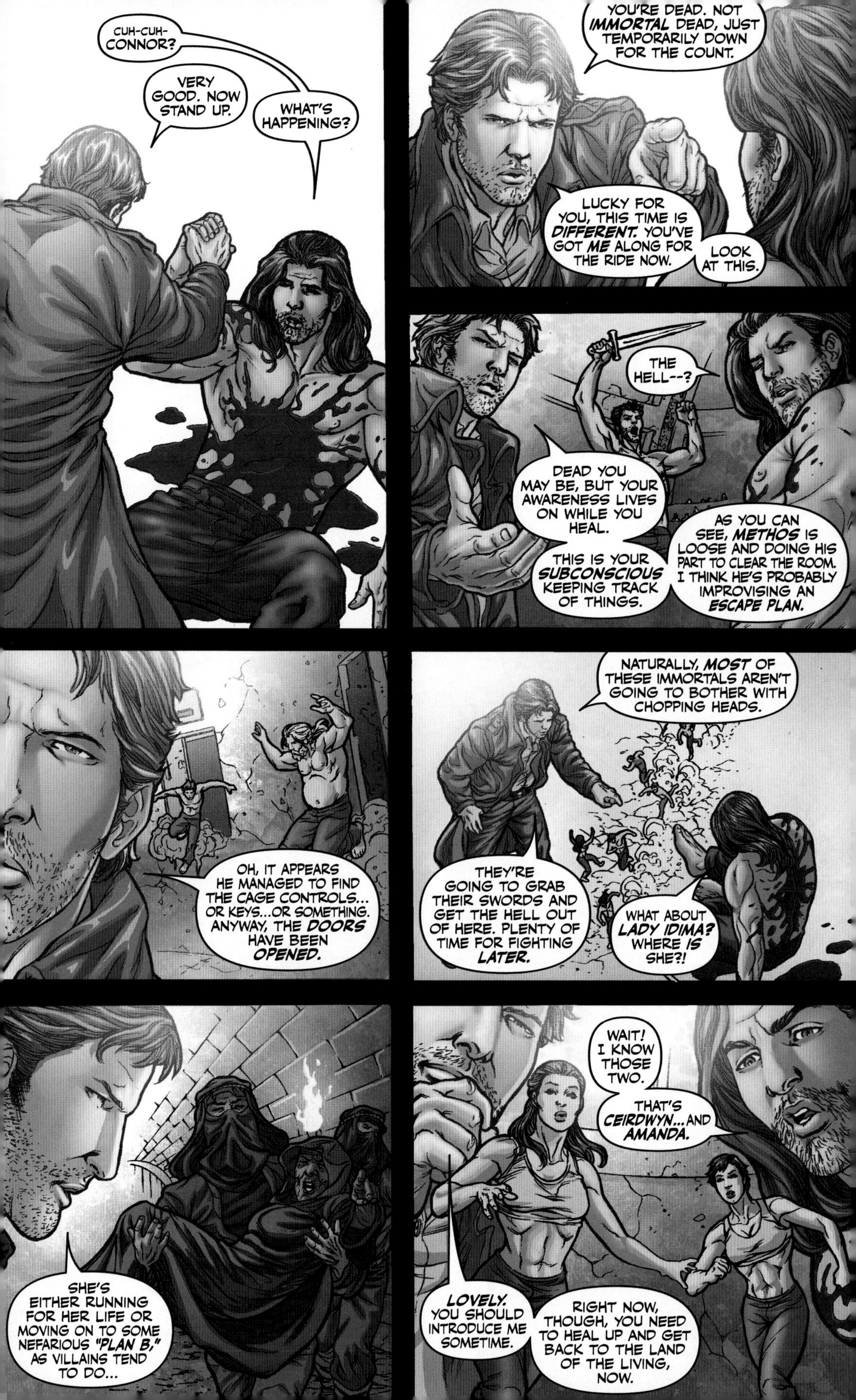
CUH-CUH-CONNOR?
VERY GOOD. NOW STAND UP.
WHAT'S HAPPENING?
YOU'RE DEAD. NOT *IMMORTAL* DEAD, JUST TEMPORARILY DOWN FOR THE COUNT.
LUCKY FOR YOU, THIS TIME IS *DIFFERENT.* YOU'VE GOT *ME* ALONG FOR THE RIDE NOW.
LOOK AT THIS.
THE HELL--?
DEAD YOU MAY BE, BUT YOUR AWARENESS LIVES ON WHILE YOU HEAL.
THIS IS YOUR *SUBCONSCIOUS* KEEPING TRACK OF THINGS.
AS YOU CAN SEE, *METHOS* IS LOOSE AND DOING HIS PART TO CLEAR THE ROOM. I THINK HE'S PROBABLY IMPROVISING AN *ESCAPE PLAN.*
OH, IT APPEARS HE MANAGED TO FIND THE CAGE CONTROLS... OR KEYS...OR SOMETHING. ANYWAY, THE *DOORS* HAVE BEEN *OPENED.*
NATURALLY, *MOST* OF THESE IMMORTALS AREN'T GOING TO BOTHER WITH CHOPPING HEADS.
THEY'RE GOING TO GRAB THEIR SWORDS AND GET THE HELL OUT OF HERE. PLENTY OF TIME FOR FIGHTING *LATER.*
WHAT ABOUT *LADY IDIMA?* WHERE *IS* SHE?!
SHE'S EITHER RUNNING FOR HER LIFE OR MOVING ON TO SOME NEFARIOUS *"PLAN B,"* AS VILLAINS TEND TO DO...
WAIT! I KNOW THOSE TWO.
THAT'S *CEIRDWYN...* AND *AMANDA.*
LOVELY. YOU SHOULD INTRODUCE ME SOMETIME.
RIGHT NOW, THOUGH, YOU NEED TO HEAL UP AND GET BACK TO THE LAND OF THE LIVING, NOW.

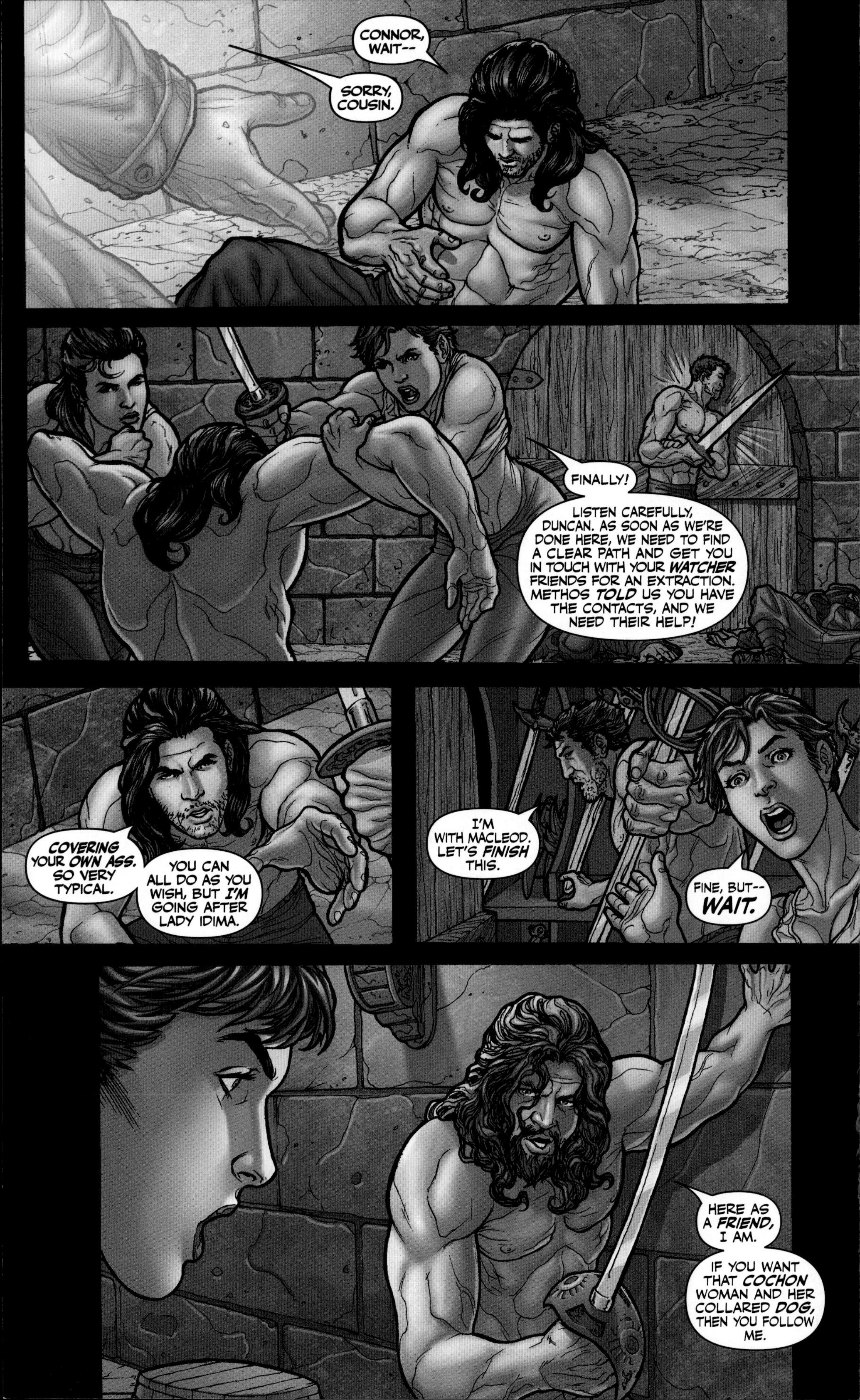
CONNOR, WAIT--
SORRY, COUSIN.
FINALLY!
LISTEN CAREFULLY, DUNCAN. AS SOON AS WE'RE DONE HERE, WE NEED TO FIND A CLEAR PATH AND GET YOU IN TOUCH WITH YOUR WATCHER FRIENDS FOR AN EXTRACTION. METHOS TOLD US YOU HAVE THE CONTACTS, AND WE NEED THEIR HELP!
COVERING YOUR OWN ASS. SO VERY TYPICAL.
YOU CAN ALL DO AS YOU WISH, BUT I'M GOING AFTER LADY IDIMA.
I'M WITH MACLEOD. LET'S FINISH THIS.
FINE, BUT-- WAIT.
HERE AS A FRIEND, I AM.
IF YOU WANT THAT COCHON WOMAN AND HER COLLARED DOG, THEN YOU FOLLOW ME.

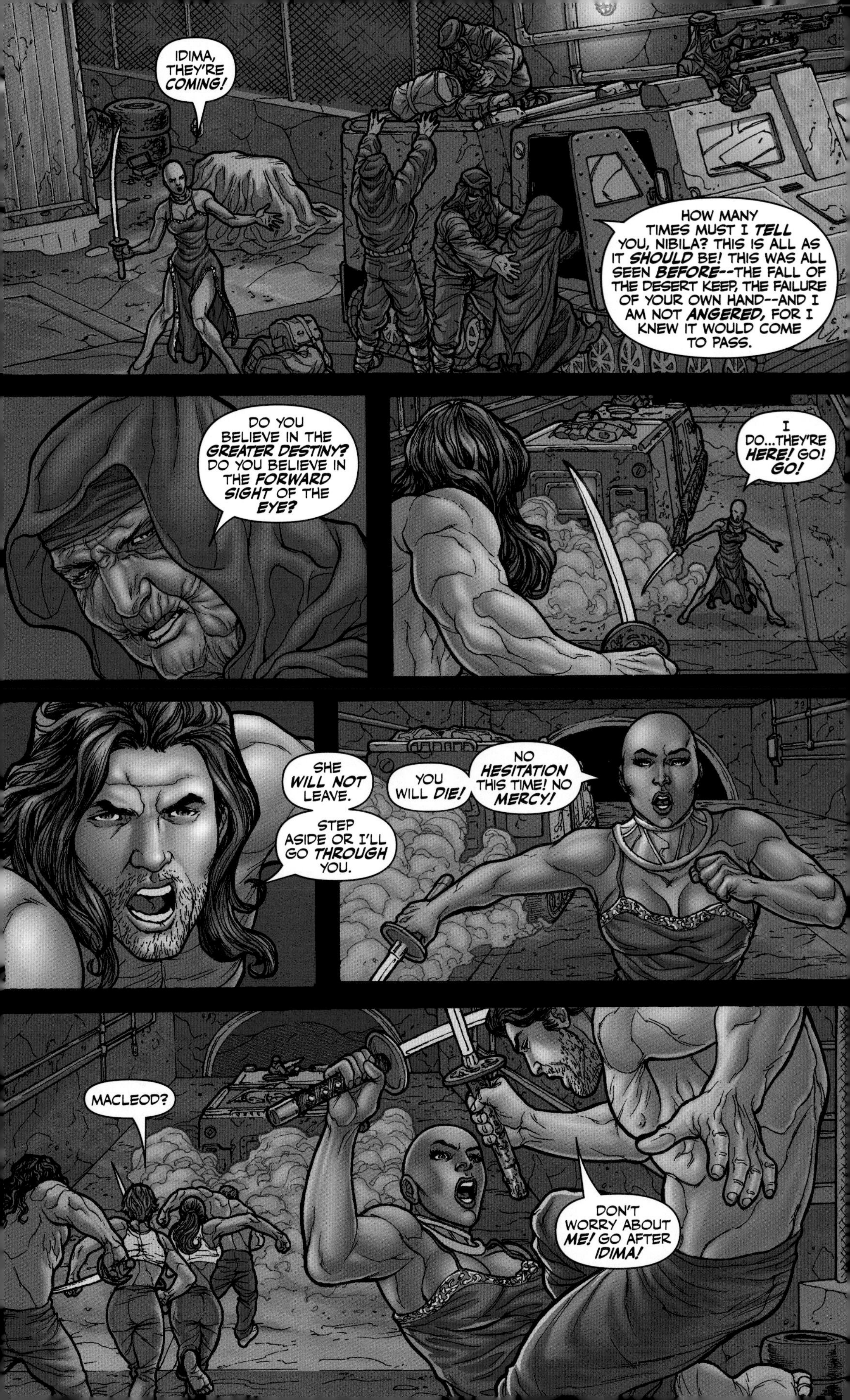
IDIMA, THEY'RE COMING!
HOW MANY TIMES MUST I TELL YOU, NIBILA? THIS IS ALL AS IT SHOULD BE! THIS WAS ALL SEEN BEFORE--THE FALL OF THE DESERT KEEP, THE FAILURE OF YOUR OWN HAND--AND I AM NOT ANGERED, FOR I KNEW IT WOULD COME TO PASS.
DO YOU BELIEVE IN THE GREATER DESTINY? DO YOU BELIEVE IN THE FORWARD SIGHT OF THE EYE?
I DO...THEY'RE HERE! GO! GO!
SHE WILL NOT LEAVE.
STEP ASIDE OR I'LL GO THROUGH YOU.
YOU WILL DIE!
NO HESITATION THIS TIME! NO MERCY!
MACLEOD?
DON'T WORRY ABOUT ME! GO AFTER IDIMA!

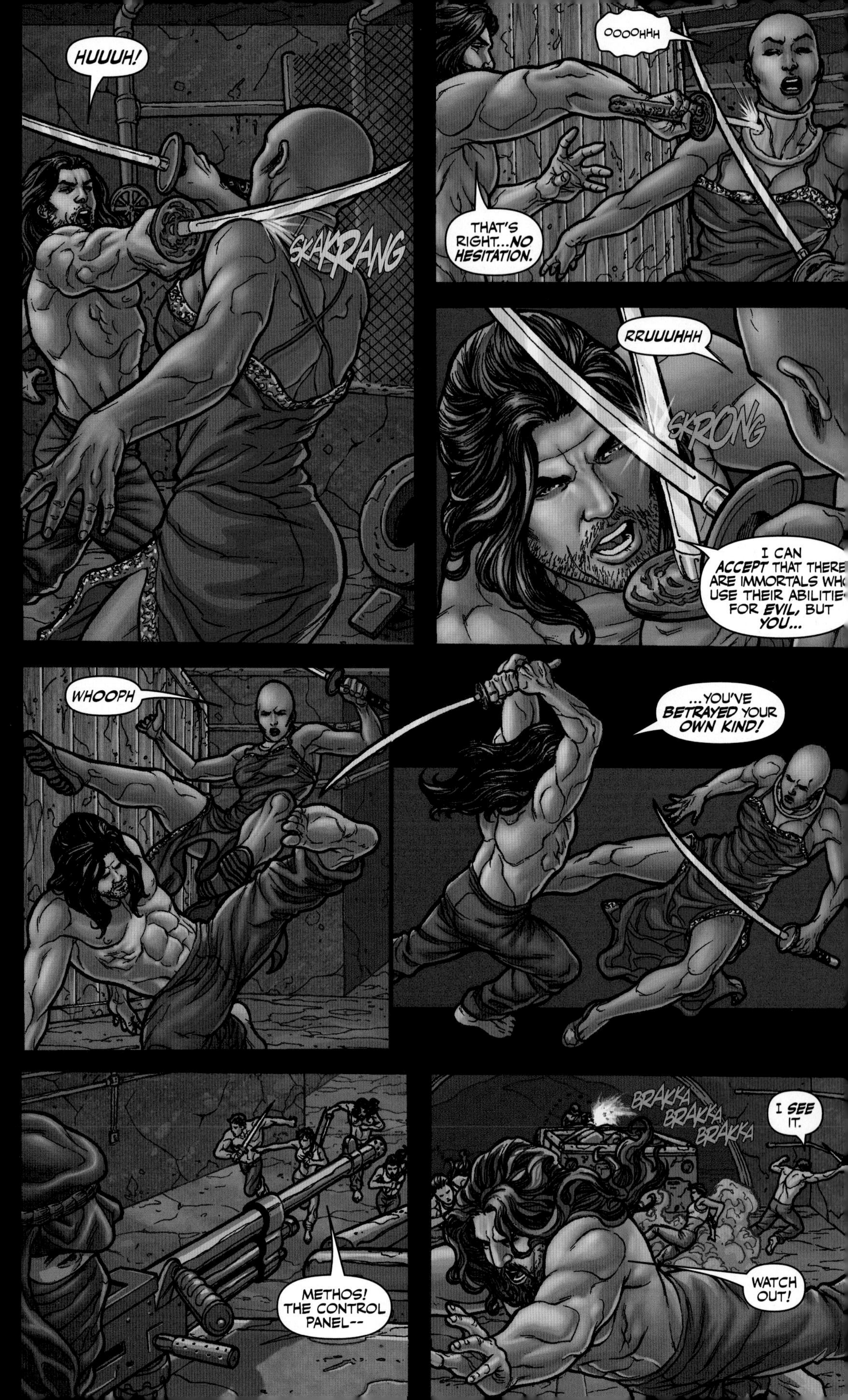
HUUUH!
SKAKRANG
OOOOHHH
THAT'S RIGHT...NO HESITATION.
RRUUUHHH
SKRONG
I CAN ACCEPT THAT THERE ARE IMMORTALS WHO USE THEIR ABILITIES FOR EVIL, BUT YOU...
WHOOPH
...YOU'VE BETRAYED YOUR OWN KIND!
METHOS! THE CONTROL PANEL--
BRAKKA BRAKKA BRAKKA
I SEE IT.
WATCH OUT!

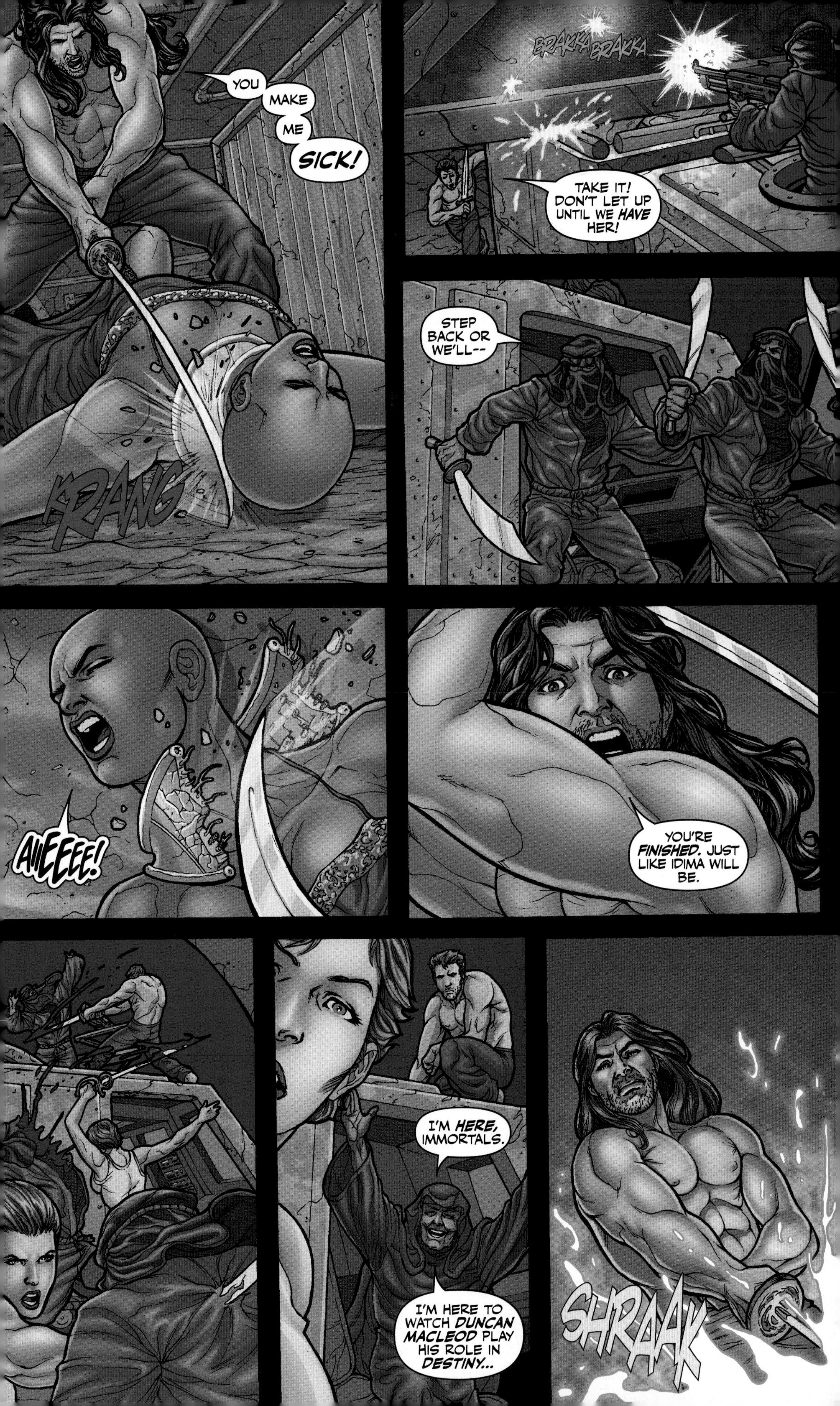
YOU MAKE ME SICK!
KRANG
BRAKKA BRAKKA
TAKE IT! DON'T LET UP UNTIL WE HAVE HER!
STEP BACK OR WE'LL--
AIIEEEE!
YOU'RE FINISHED. JUST LIKE IDIMA WILL BE.
I'M HERE, IMMORTALS.
I'M HERE TO WATCH DUNCAN MACLEOD PLAY HIS ROLE IN DESTINY...
SHRAAK

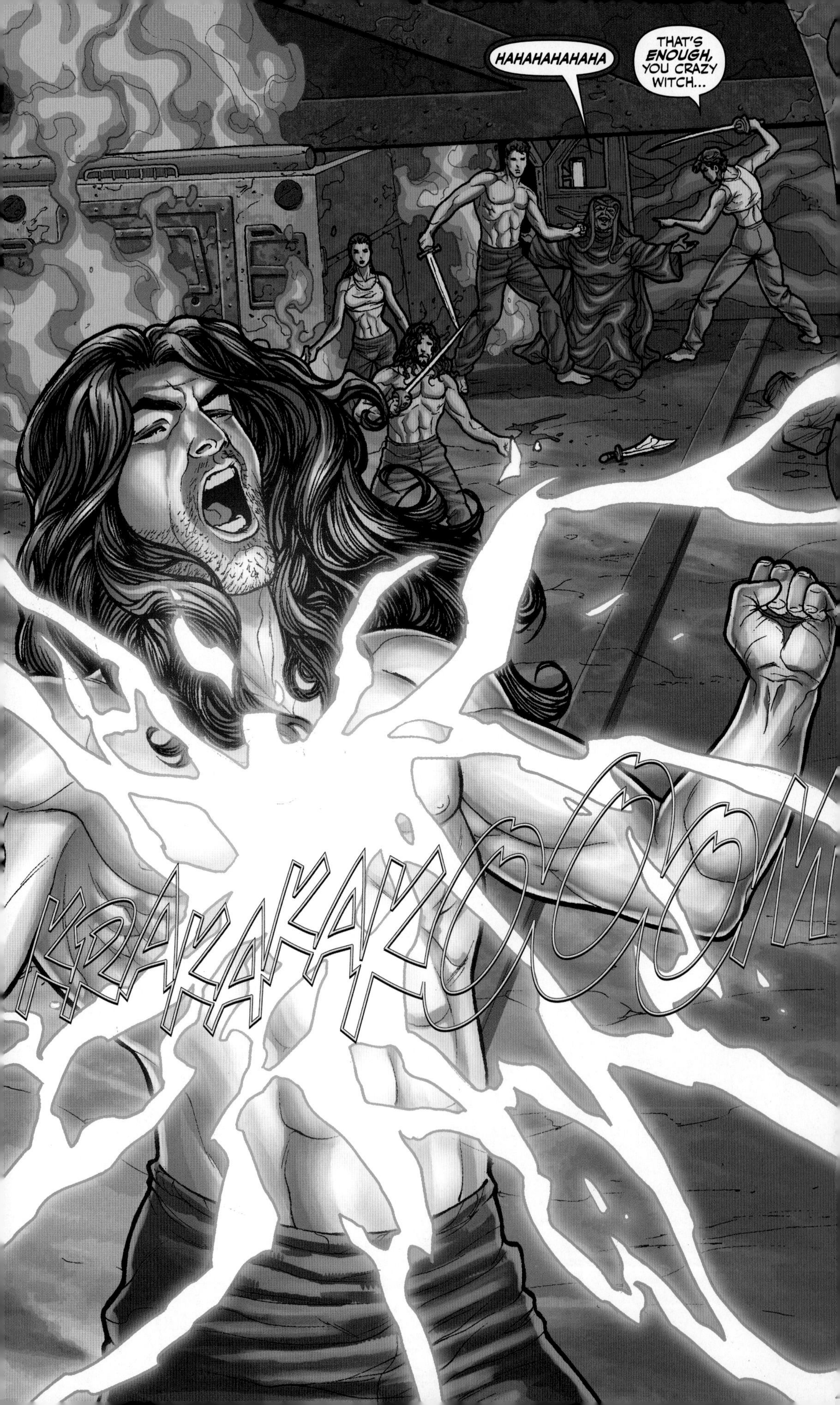
HAHAHAHAHAHA
THAT'S ENOUGH, YOU CRAZY WITCH...
KRAKAKAKOOOOM

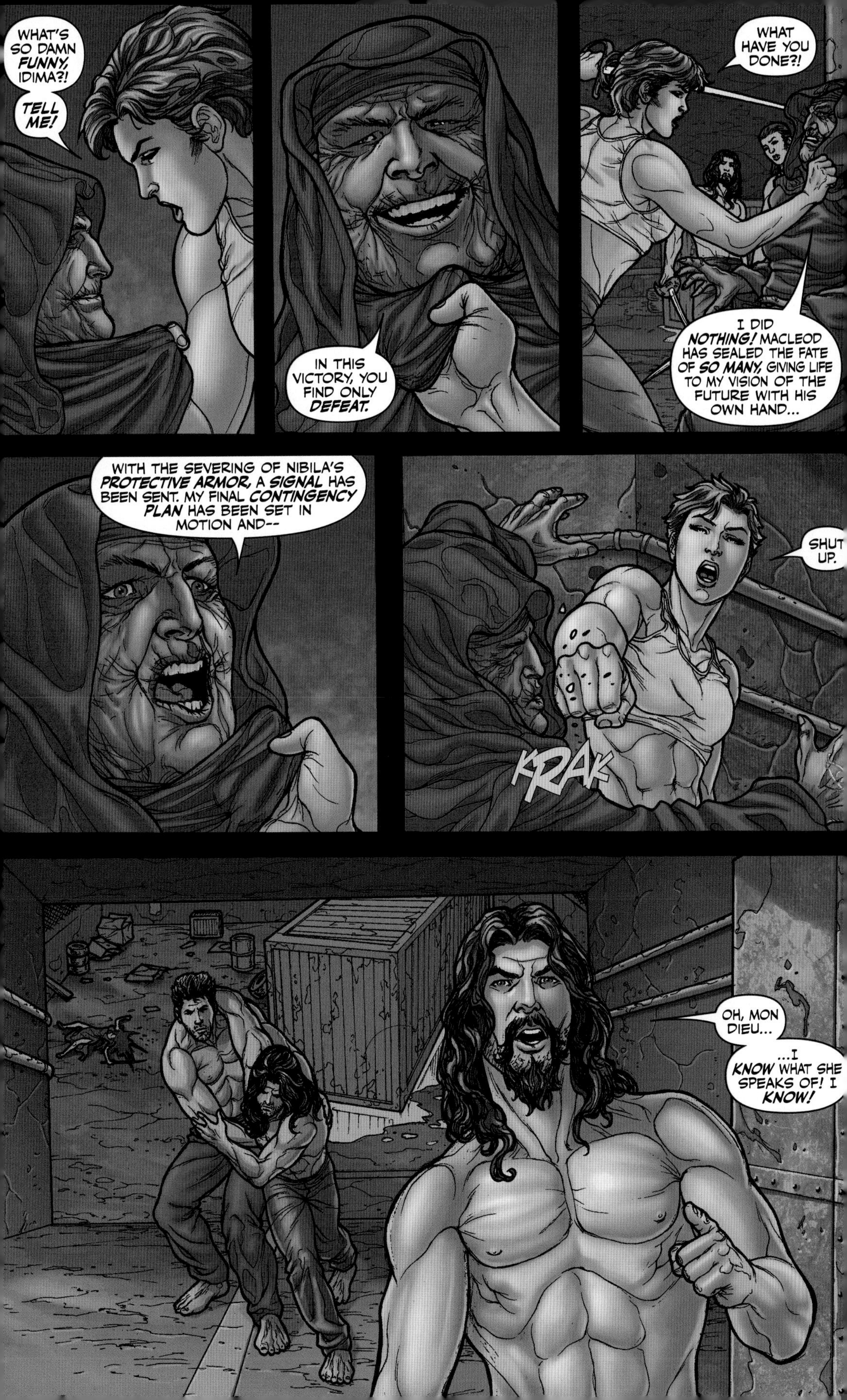
WHAT'S SO DAMN FUNNY, IDIMA?!
TELL ME!
IN THIS VICTORY, YOU FIND ONLY DEFEAT.
WHAT HAVE YOU DONE?!
I DID NOTHING! MACLEOD HAS SEALED THE FATE OF SO MANY, GIVING LIFE TO MY VISION OF THE FUTURE WITH HIS OWN HAND...
WITH THE SEVERING OF NIBILA'S PROTECTIVE ARMOR, A SIGNAL HAS BEEN SENT. MY FINAL CONTINGENCY PLAN HAS BEEN SET IN MOTION AND--
SHUT UP.
KRAK
OH, MON DIEU...
...I KNOW WHAT SHE SPEAKS OF! I KNOW!

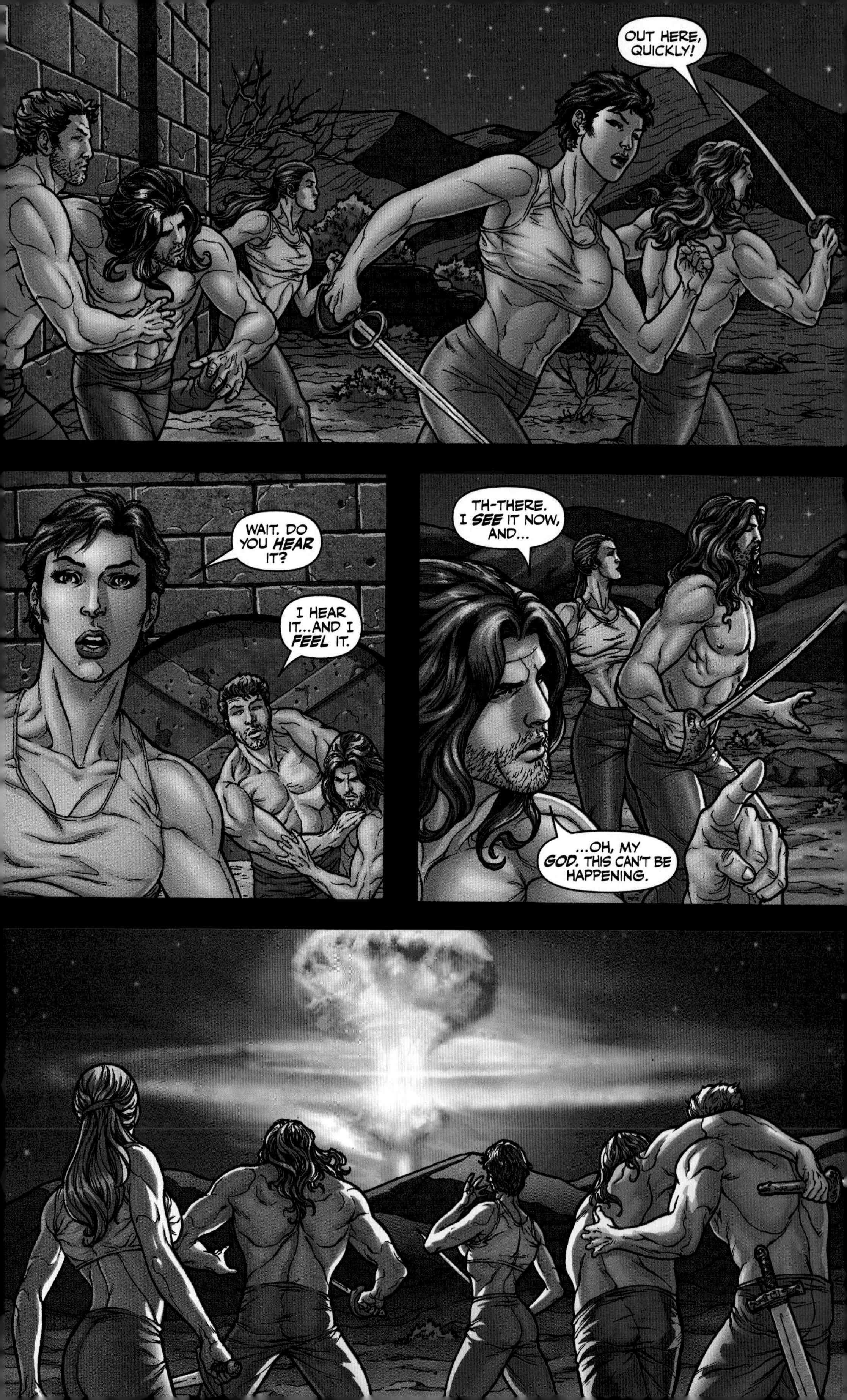
OUT HERE, QUICKLY!
WAIT. DO YOU HEAR IT?
I HEAR IT...AND I FEEL IT.
TH-THERE. I SEE IT NOW, AND...
...OH, MY GOD. THIS CAN'T BE HAPPENING.

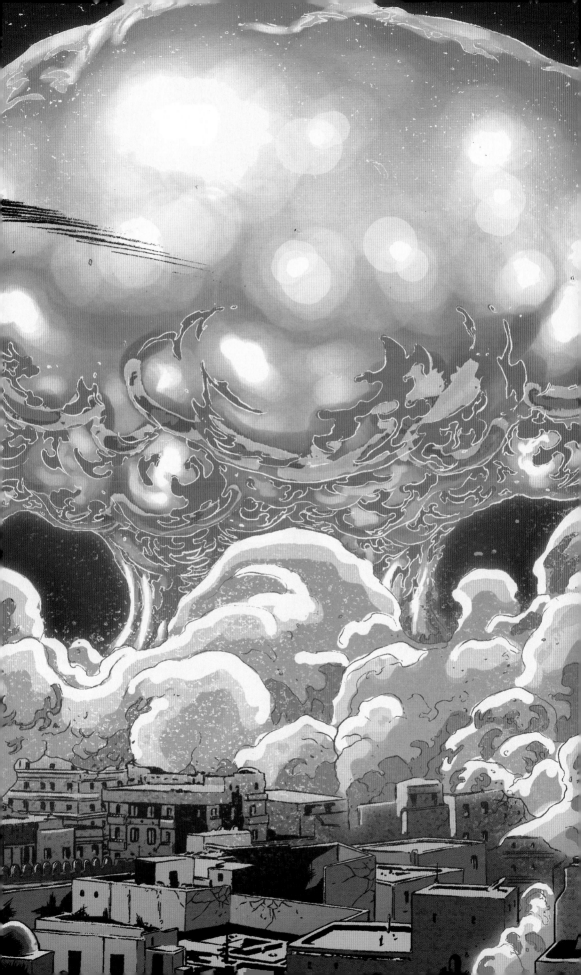

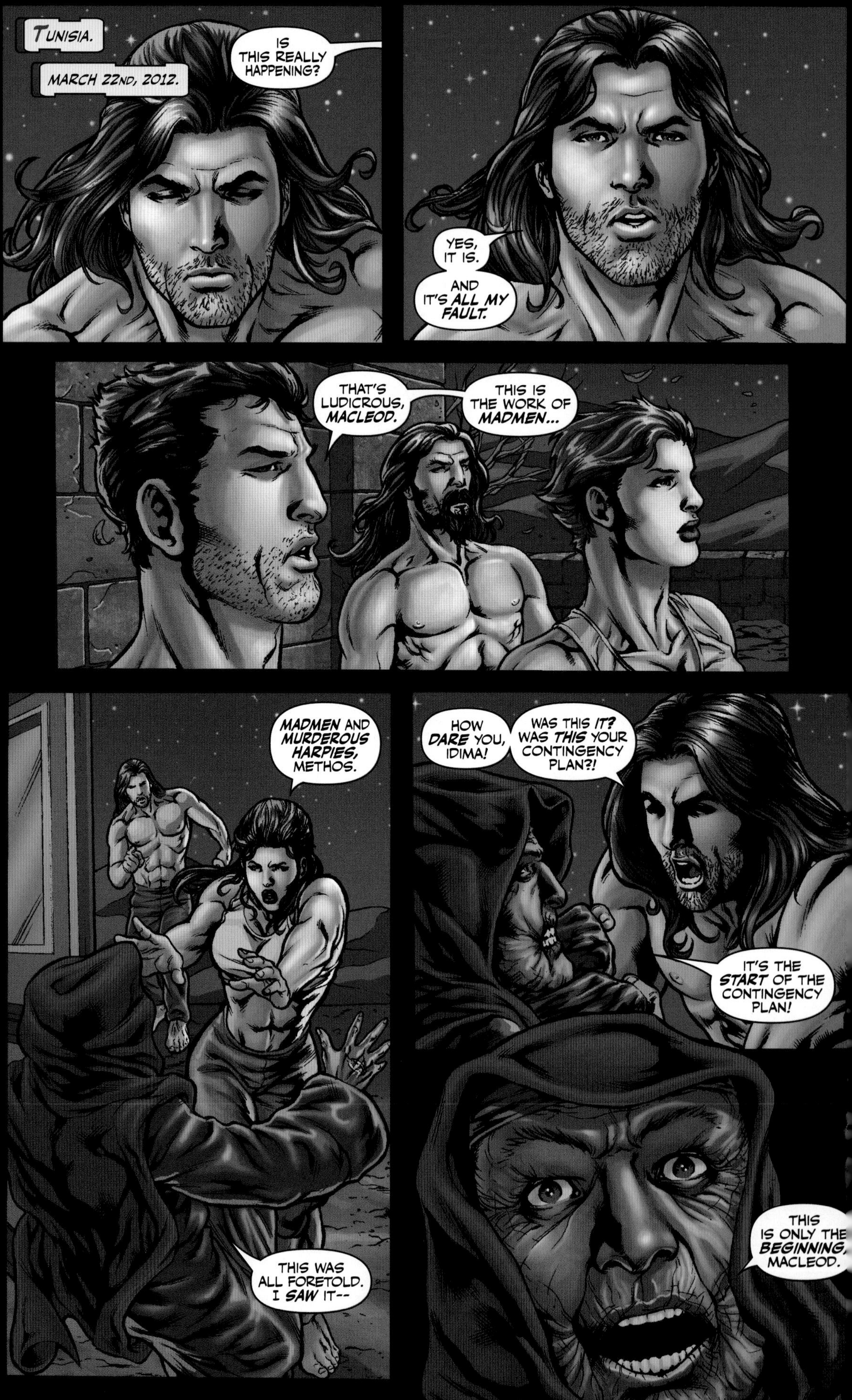
TUNISIA.
MARCH 22ND, 2012.
IS THIS REALLY HAPPENING?
YES, IT IS.
AND IT'S ALL MY FAULT.
THAT'S LUDICROUS, MACLEOD.
THIS IS THE WORK OF MADMEN...
MADMEN AND MURDEROUS HARPIES, METHOS.
THIS WAS ALL FORETOLD. I SAW IT--
HOW DARE YOU, IDIMA!
WAS THIS IT? WAS THIS YOUR CONTINGENCY PLAN?!
IT'S THE START OF THE CONTINGENCY PLAN!
THIS IS ONLY THE BEGINNING, MACLEOD.

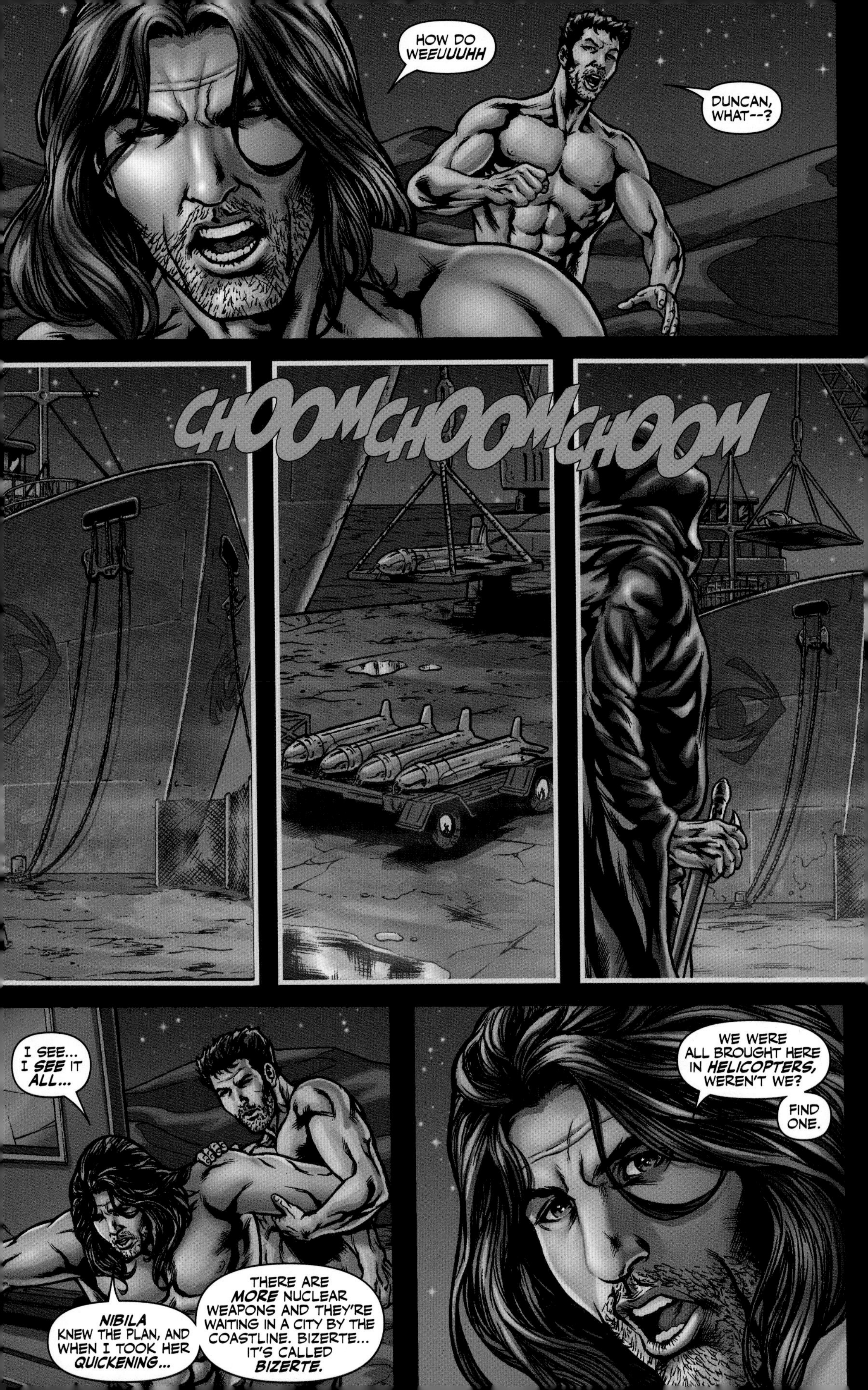

HOW DO WEEUUUHH
DUNCAN, WHAT--?
CHOOM CHOOM CHOOM
I SEE... I *SEE* IT *ALL*...
NIBILA KNEW THE PLAN, AND WHEN I TOOK HER *QUICKENING*...
THERE ARE *MORE* NUCLEAR WEAPONS AND THEY'RE WAITING IN A CITY BY THE COASTLINE. BIZERTE... IT'S CALLED *BIZERTE*.
WE WERE ALL BROUGHT HERE IN *HELICOPTERS*, WEREN'T WE?
FIND ONE.

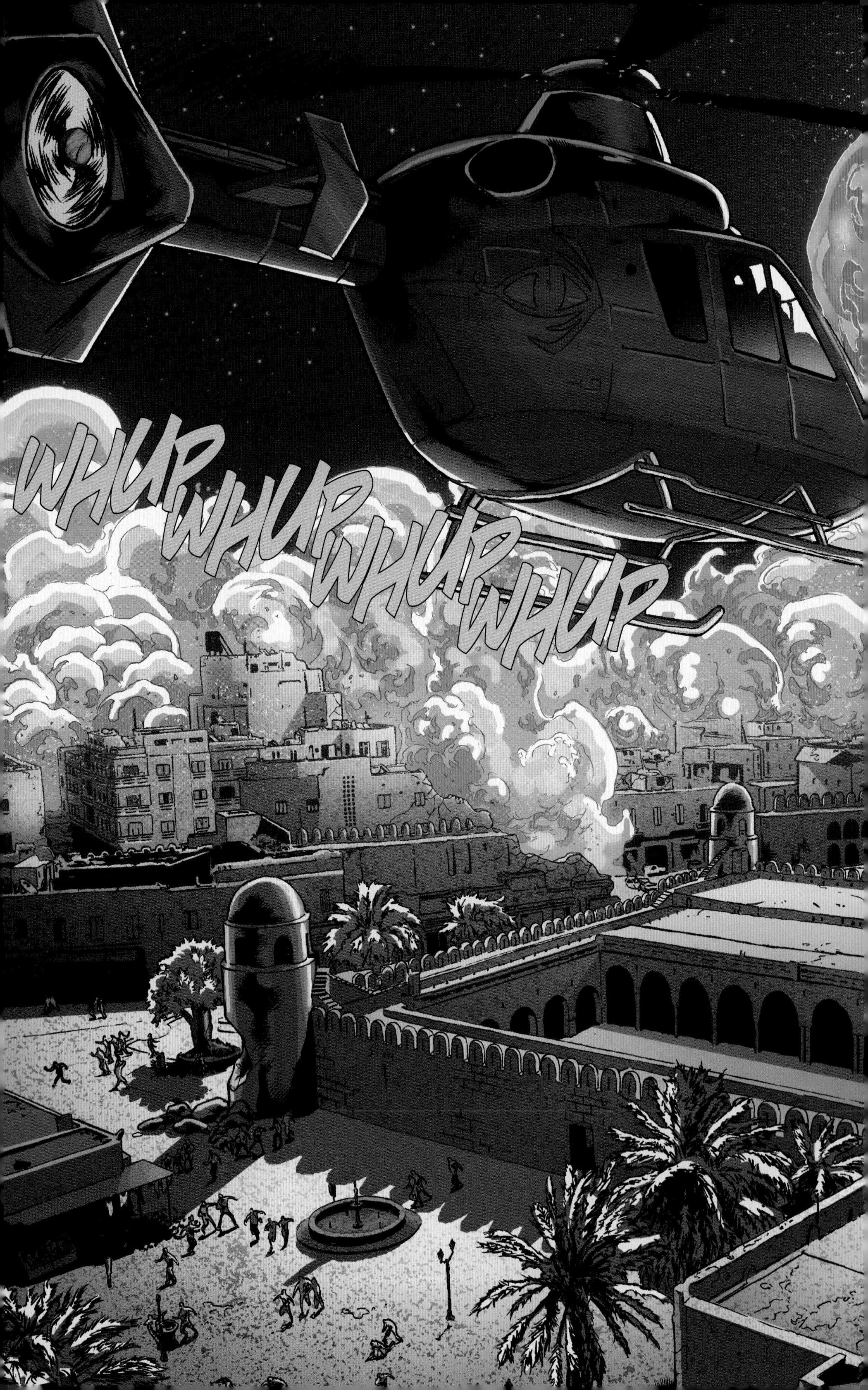
WHUP WHUP WHUP WHUP

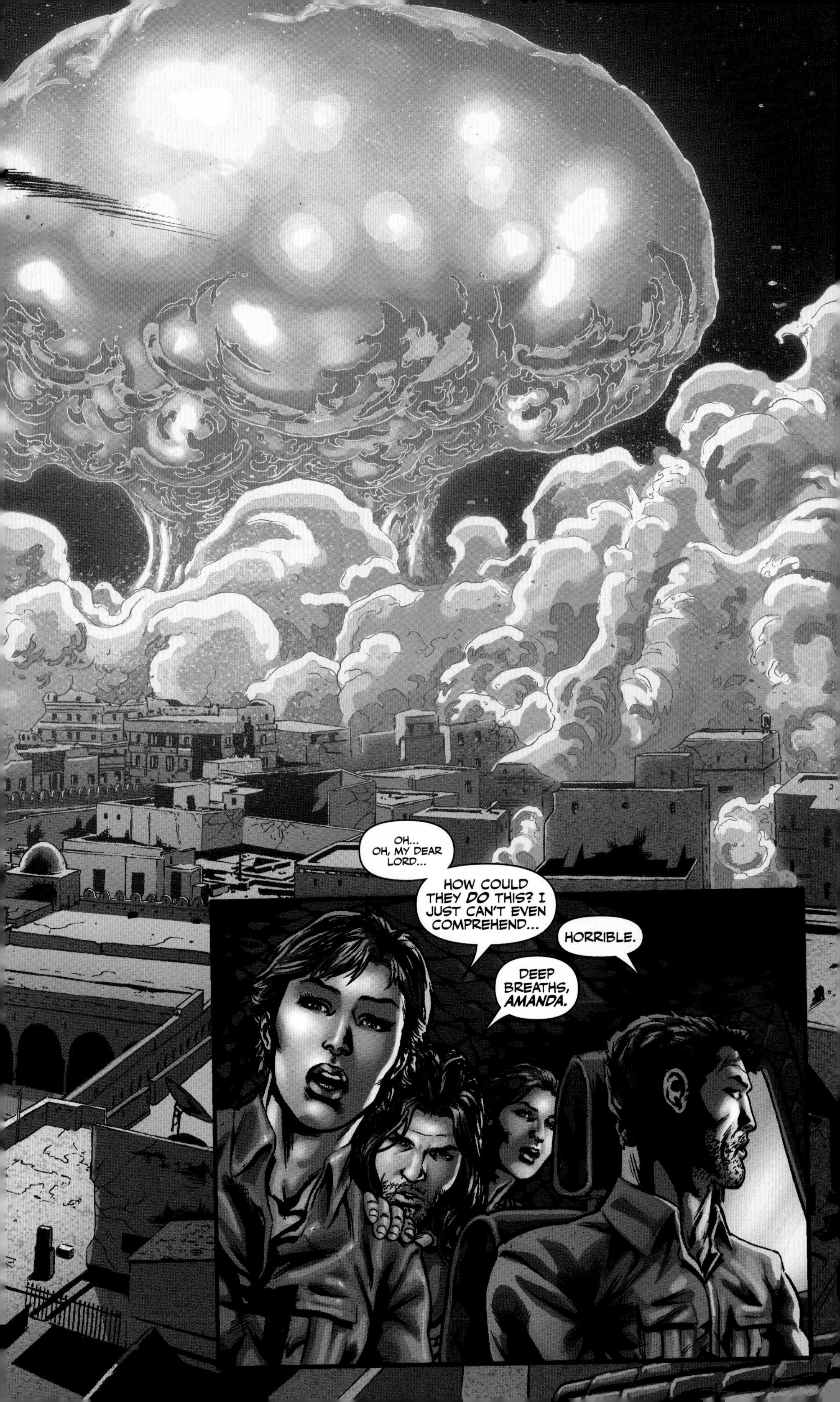
OH...
OH, MY DEAR LORD...
HOW COULD THEY DO THIS? I JUST CAN'T EVEN COMPREHEND...
HORRIBLE.
DEEP BREATHS, AMANDA.

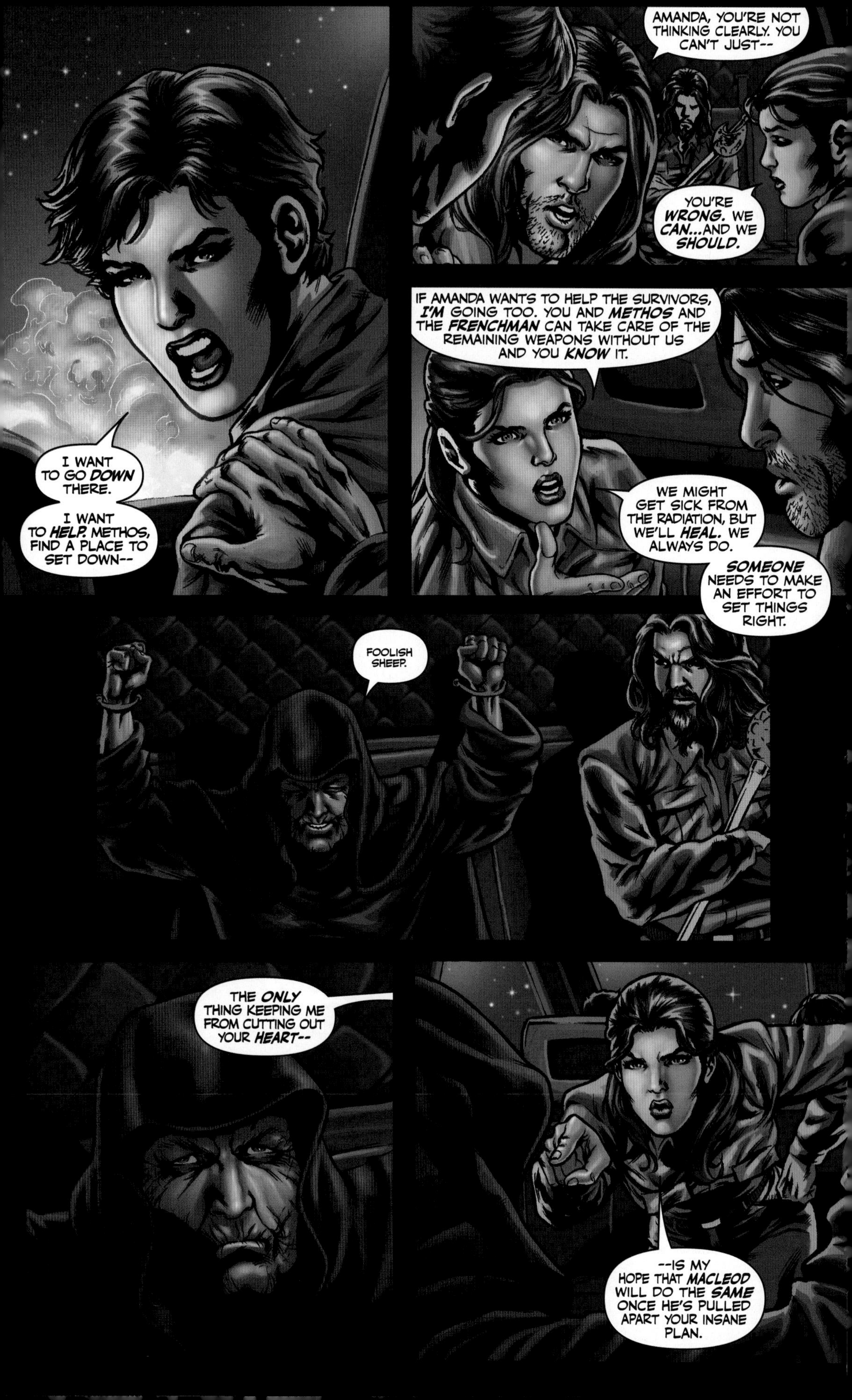

I WANT TO GO DOWN THERE.
I WANT TO HELP. METHOS, FIND A PLACE TO SET DOWN--
AMANDA, YOU'RE NOT THINKING CLEARLY. YOU CAN'T JUST--
YOU'RE WRONG. WE CAN...AND WE SHOULD.
IF AMANDA WANTS TO HELP THE SURVIVORS, I'M GOING TOO. YOU AND METHOS AND THE FRENCHMAN CAN TAKE CARE OF THE REMAINING WEAPONS WITHOUT US AND YOU KNOW IT.
WE MIGHT GET SICK FROM THE RADIATION, BUT WE'LL HEAL. WE ALWAYS DO.
SOMEONE NEEDS TO MAKE AN EFFORT TO SET THINGS RIGHT.
FOOLISH SHEEP.
THE ONLY THING KEEPING ME FROM CUTTING OUT YOUR HEART--
--IS MY HOPE THAT MACLEOD WILL DO THE SAME ONCE HE'S PULLED APART YOUR INSANE PLAN.

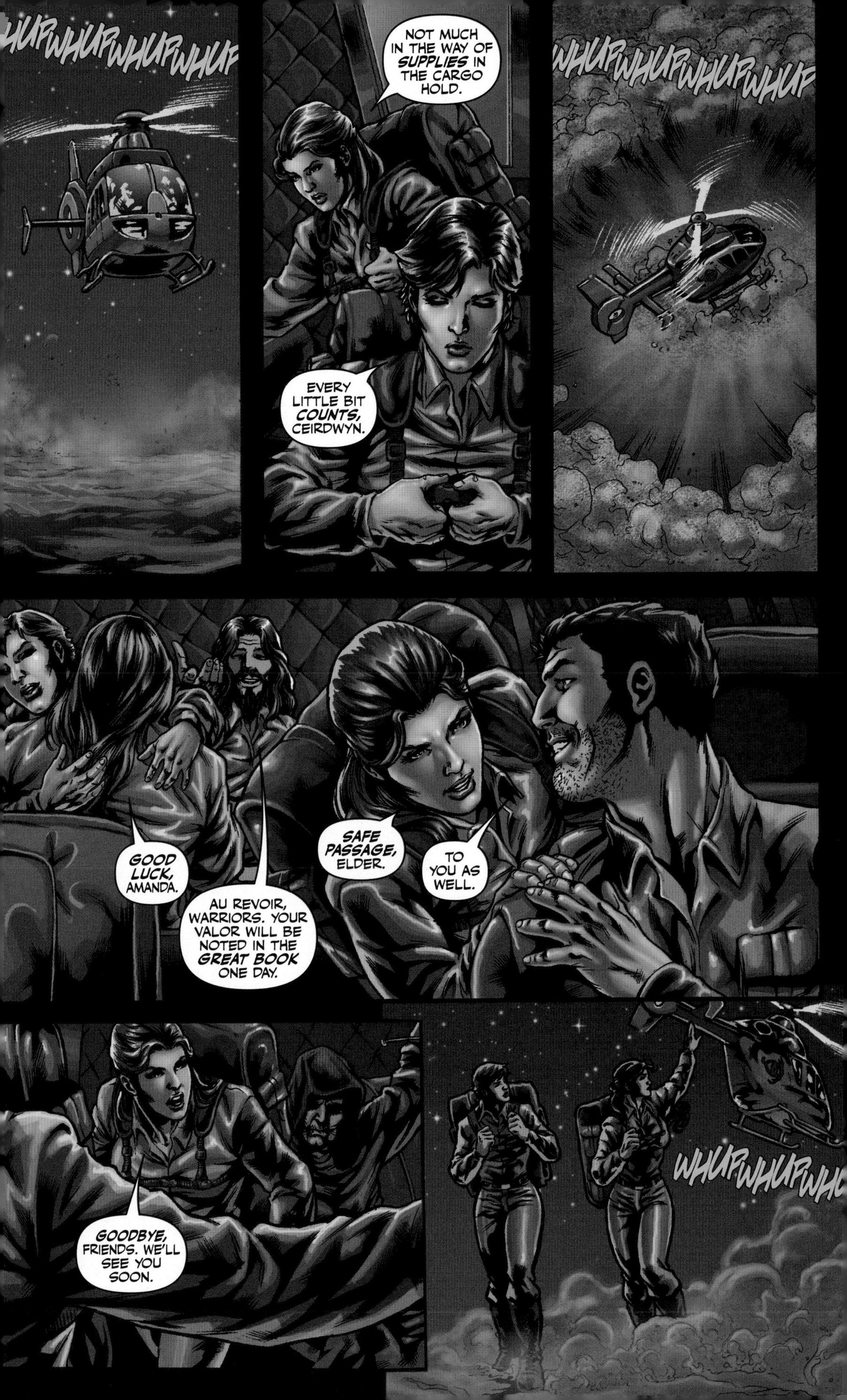
WHUP WHUP WHUP WHUP
NOT MUCH IN THE WAY OF SUPPLIES IN THE CARGO HOLD.
EVERY LITTLE BIT COUNTS, CEIRDWYN.
WHUP WHUP WHUP WHUP
GOOD LUCK, AMANDA.
AU REVOIR, WARRIORS. YOUR VALOR WILL BE NOTED IN THE GREAT BOOK ONE DAY.
SAFE PASSAGE, ELDER.
TO YOU AS WELL.
GOODBYE, FRIENDS. WE'LL SEE YOU SOON.
WHUP WHUP WHU

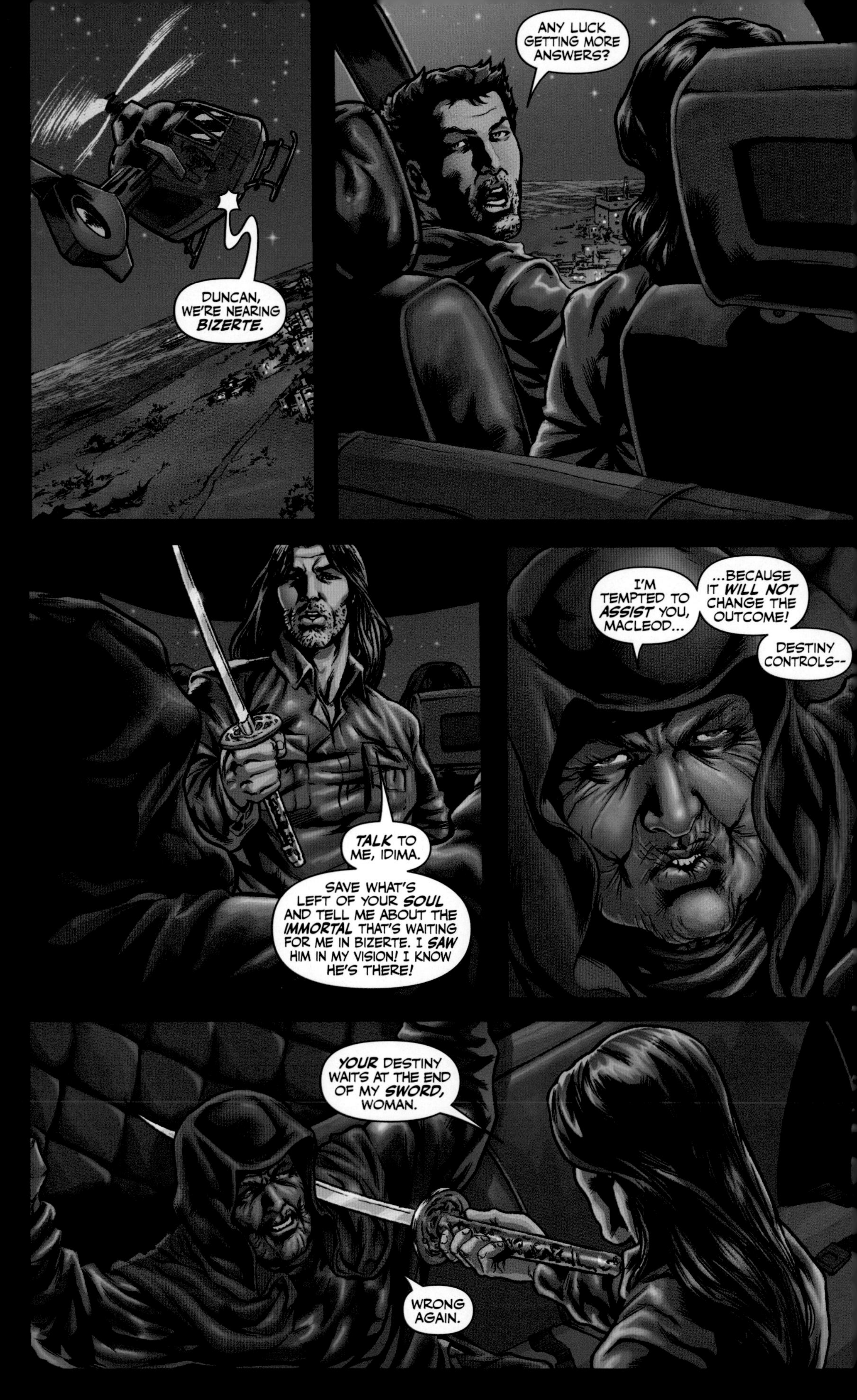
DUNCAN, WE'RE NEARING *BIZERTE.*
ANY LUCK GETTING MORE ANSWERS?
TALK TO ME, IDIMA.
SAVE WHAT'S LEFT OF YOUR *SOUL* AND TELL ME ABOUT THE *IMMORTAL* THAT'S WAITING FOR ME IN BIZERTE. I *SAW* HIM IN MY VISION! I KNOW HE'S THERE!
I'M TEMPTED TO *ASSIST* YOU, MACLEOD...
...BECAUSE IT *WILL NOT* CHANGE THE OUTCOME!
DESTINY CONTROLS--
YOUR DESTINY WAITS AT THE END OF MY *SWORD,* WOMAN.
WRONG AGAIN.

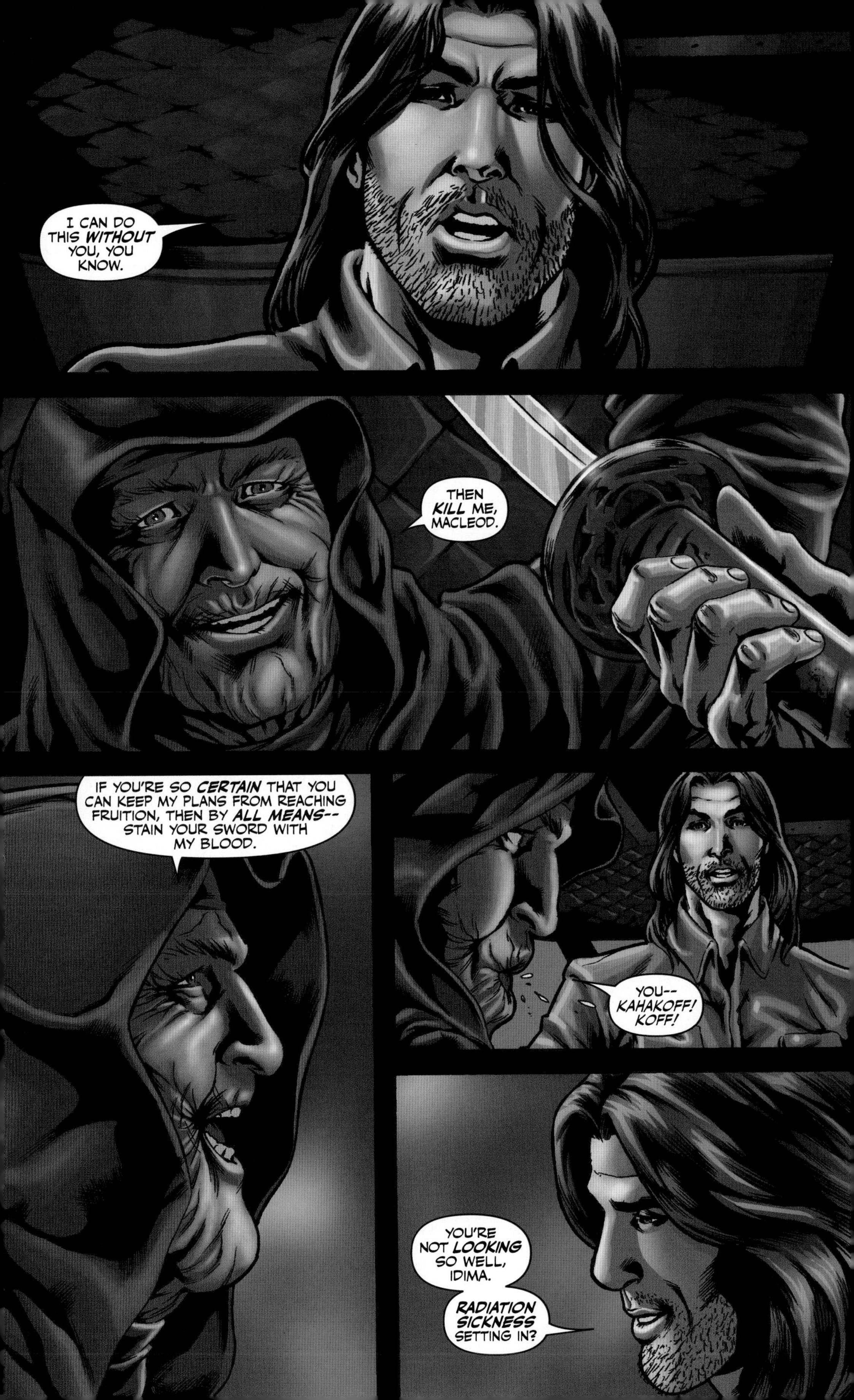
I CAN DO THIS *WITHOUT* YOU, YOU KNOW.
THEN *KILL* ME, MACLEOD.
IF YOU'RE SO *CERTAIN* THAT YOU CAN KEEP MY PLANS FROM REACHING FRUITION, THEN BY *ALL MEANS*-- STAIN YOUR SWORD WITH MY BLOOD.
YOU-- *KAHAKOFF! KOFF!*
YOU'RE NOT *LOOKING* SO WELL, IDIMA.
RADIATION SICKNESS SETTING IN?

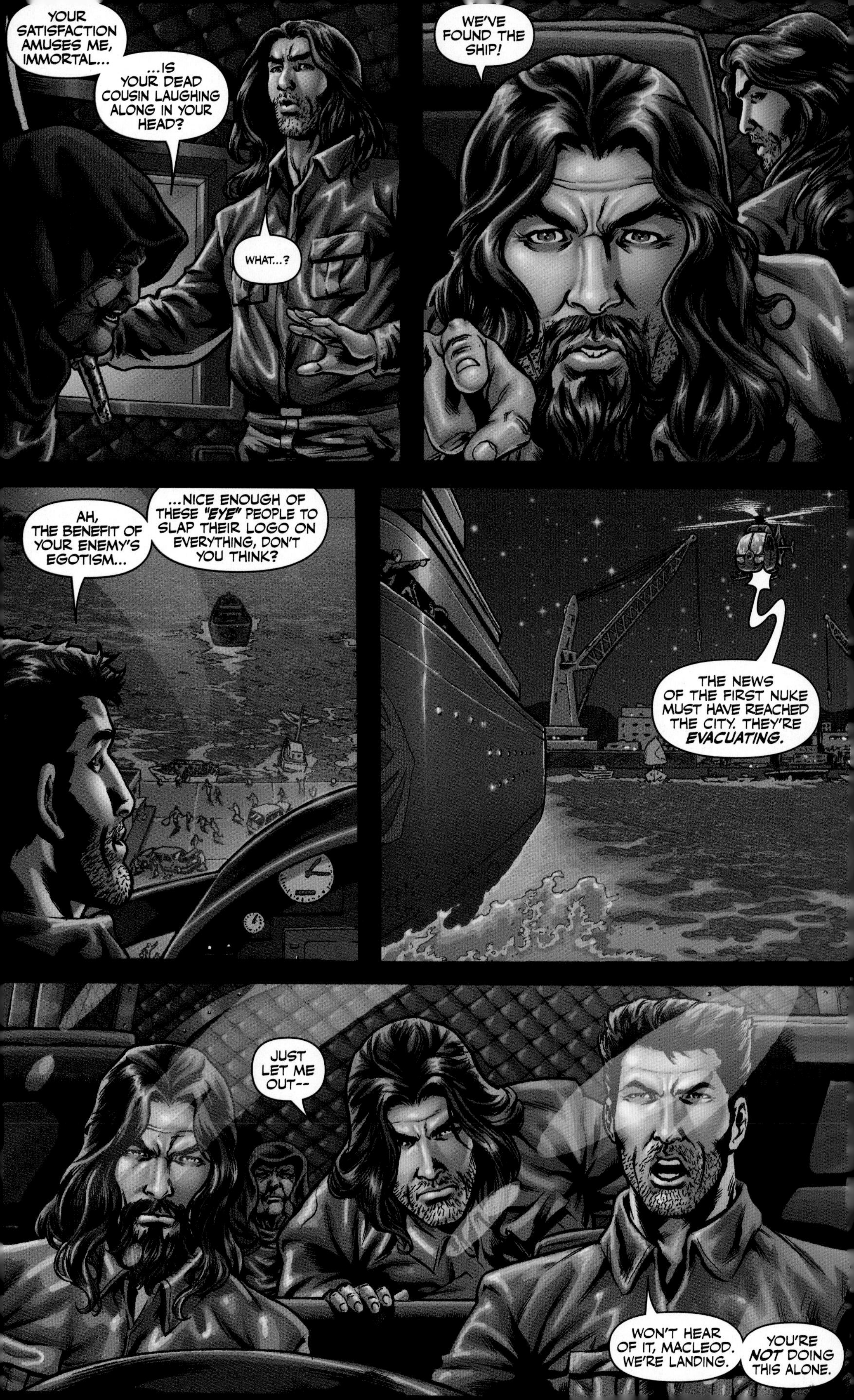
YOUR SATISFACTION AMUSES ME, IMMORTAL...
...IS YOUR DEAD COUSIN LAUGHING ALONG IN YOUR HEAD?
WHAT...?
WE'VE FOUND THE SHIP!
AH, THE BENEFIT OF YOUR ENEMY'S EGOTISM...
...NICE ENOUGH OF THESE "EYE" PEOPLE TO SLAP THEIR LOGO ON EVERYTHING, DON'T YOU THINK?
THE NEWS OF THE FIRST NUKE MUST HAVE REACHED THE CITY. THEY'RE EVACUATING.
JUST LET ME OUT--
WON'T HEAR OF IT, MACLEOD. WE'RE LANDING.
YOU'RE NOT DOING THIS ALONE.

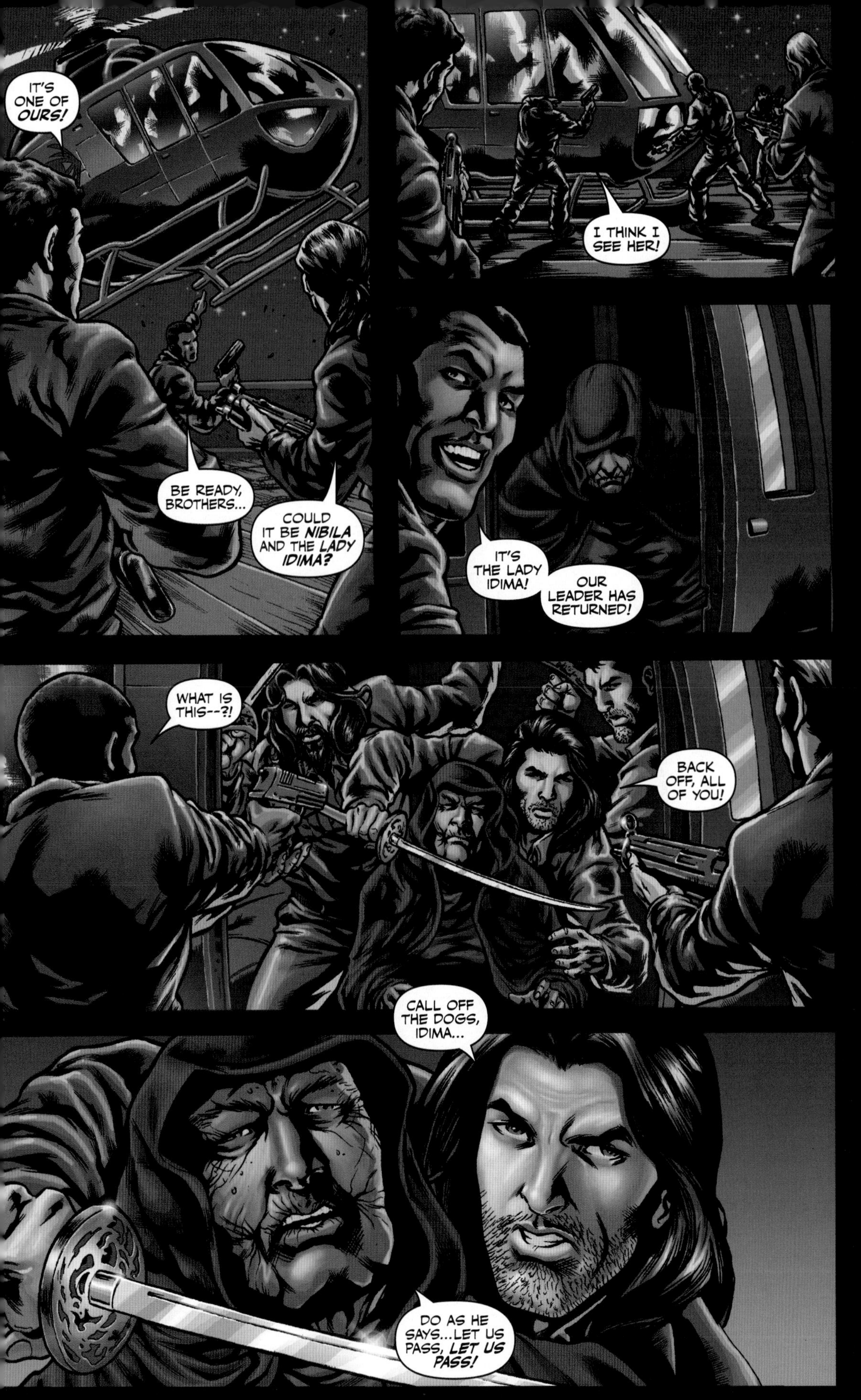
IT'S ONE OF *OURS!*
I THINK I SEE HER!
BE READY, BROTHERS...
COULD IT BE *NIBILA* AND THE *LADY IDIMA?*
IT'S THE LADY IDIMA!
OUR LEADER HAS RETURNED!
WHAT IS THIS--?!
BACK OFF, ALL OF YOU!
CALL OFF THE DOGS, IDIMA...
DO AS HE SAYS...LET US PASS, *LET US PASS!*

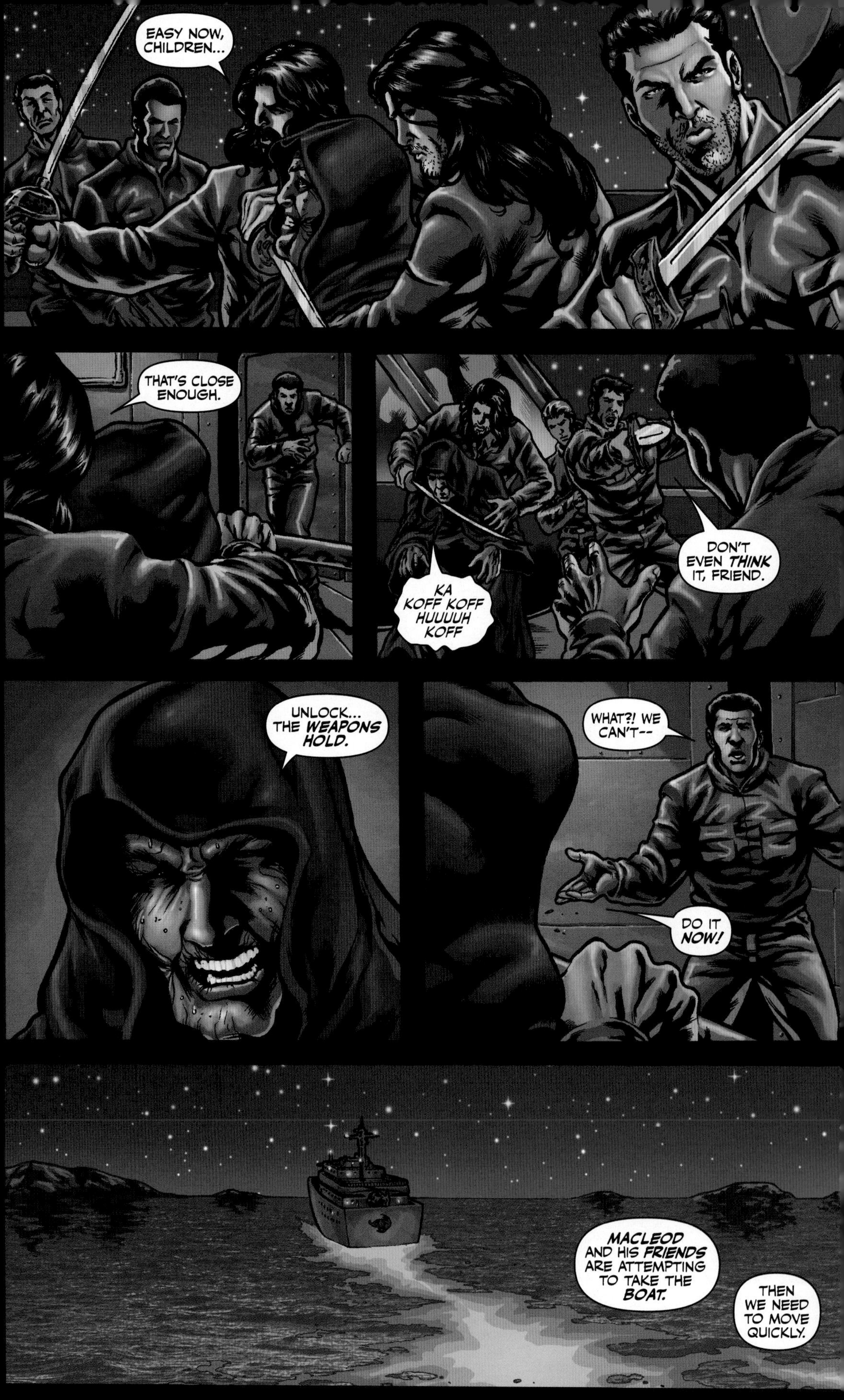
EASY NOW, CHILDREN...
THAT'S CLOSE ENOUGH.
KA KOFF KOFF HUUUUH KOFF
DON'T EVEN THINK IT, FRIEND.
UNLOCK... THE WEAPONS HOLD.
WHAT?! WE CAN'T--
DO IT NOW!
MACLEOD AND HIS FRIENDS ARE ATTEMPTING TO TAKE THE BOAT.
THEN WE NEED TO MOVE QUICKLY.

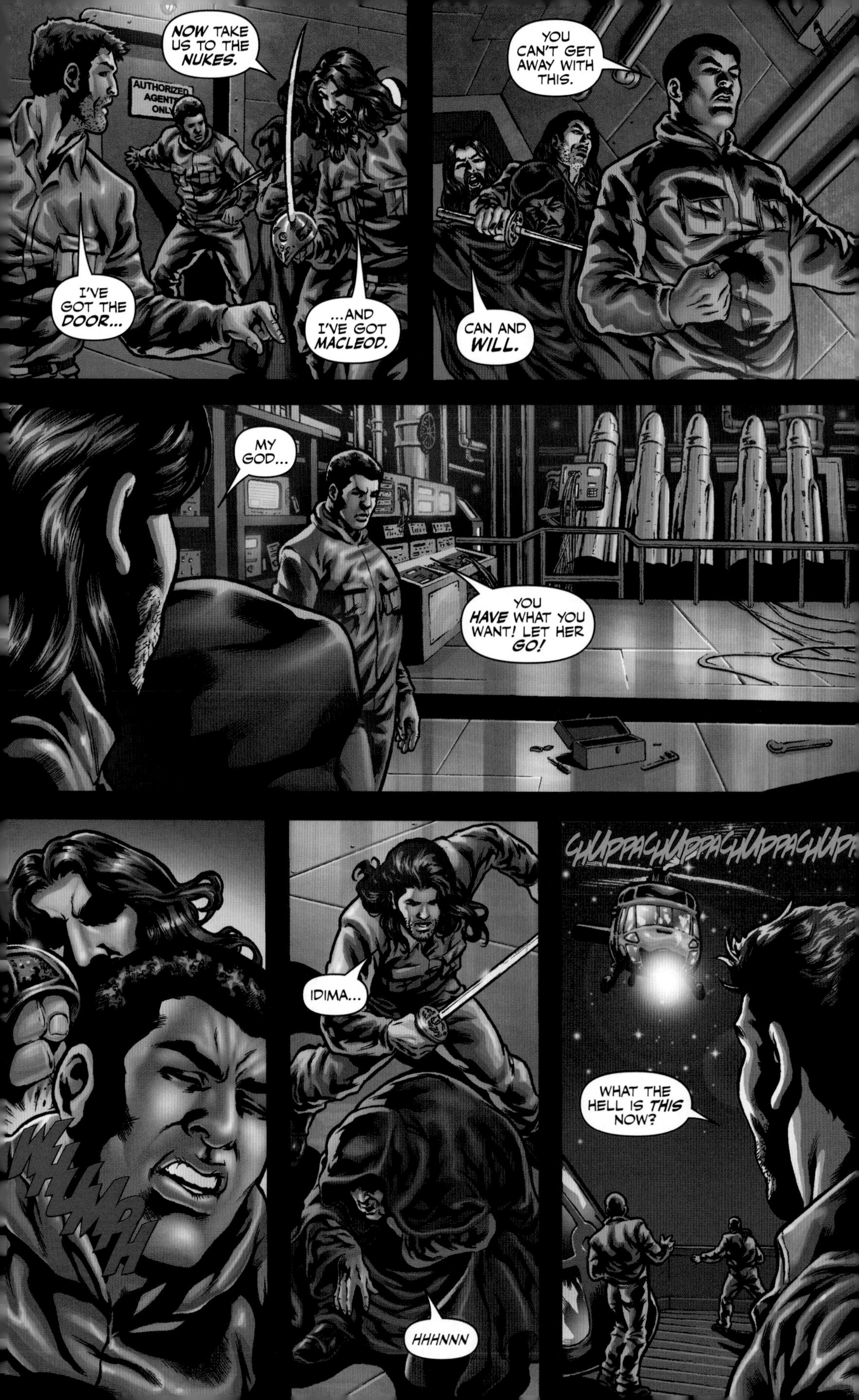
NOW TAKE US TO THE NUKES.
I'VE GOT THE DOOR...
...AND I'VE GOT MACLEOD.
YOU CAN'T GET AWAY WITH THIS.
CAN AND WILL.
MY GOD...
YOU HAVE WHAT YOU WANT! LET HER GO!
IDIMA...
HHHNNN
CHUPPACHUPPACHUPPACHUPP
WHAT THE HELL IS THIS NOW?

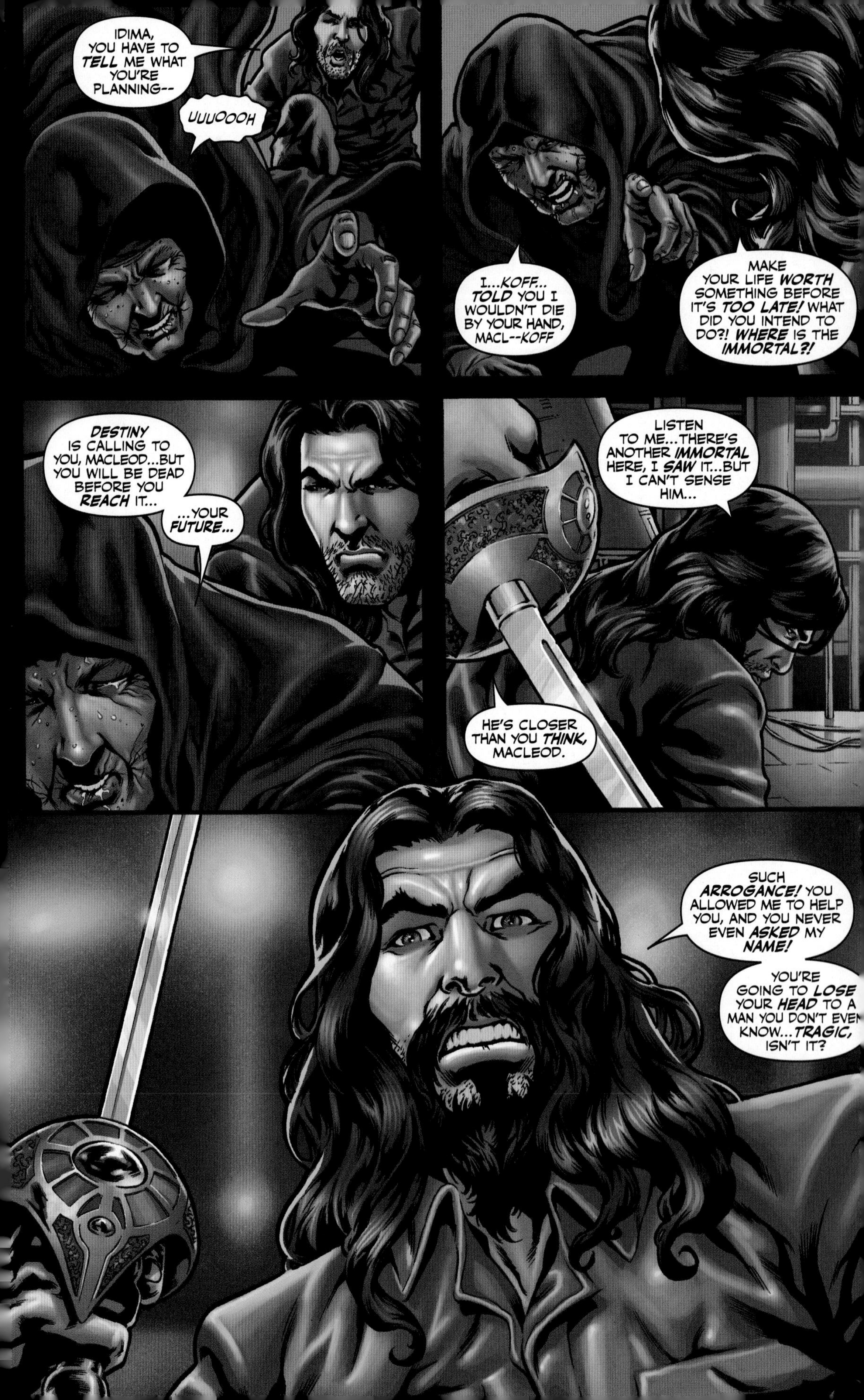
IDIMA, YOU HAVE TO TELL ME WHAT YOU'RE PLANNING--
UUUOOOH
I...KOFF... TOLD YOU I WOULDN'T DIE BY YOUR HAND, MACL--KOFF
MAKE YOUR LIFE WORTH SOMETHING BEFORE IT'S TOO LATE! WHAT DID YOU INTEND TO DO?! WHERE IS THE IMMORTAL?!
DESTINY IS CALLING TO YOU, MACLEOD...BUT YOU WILL BE DEAD BEFORE YOU REACH IT...
...YOUR FUTURE...
LISTEN TO ME...THERE'S ANOTHER IMMORTAL HERE, I SAW IT...BUT I CAN'T SENSE HIM...
HE'S CLOSER THAN YOU THINK, MACLEOD.
SUCH ARROGANCE! YOU ALLOWED ME TO HELP YOU, AND YOU NEVER EVEN ASKED MY NAME!
YOU'RE GOING TO LOSE YOUR HEAD TO A MAN YOU DON'T EVEN KNOW...TRAGIC, ISN'T IT?

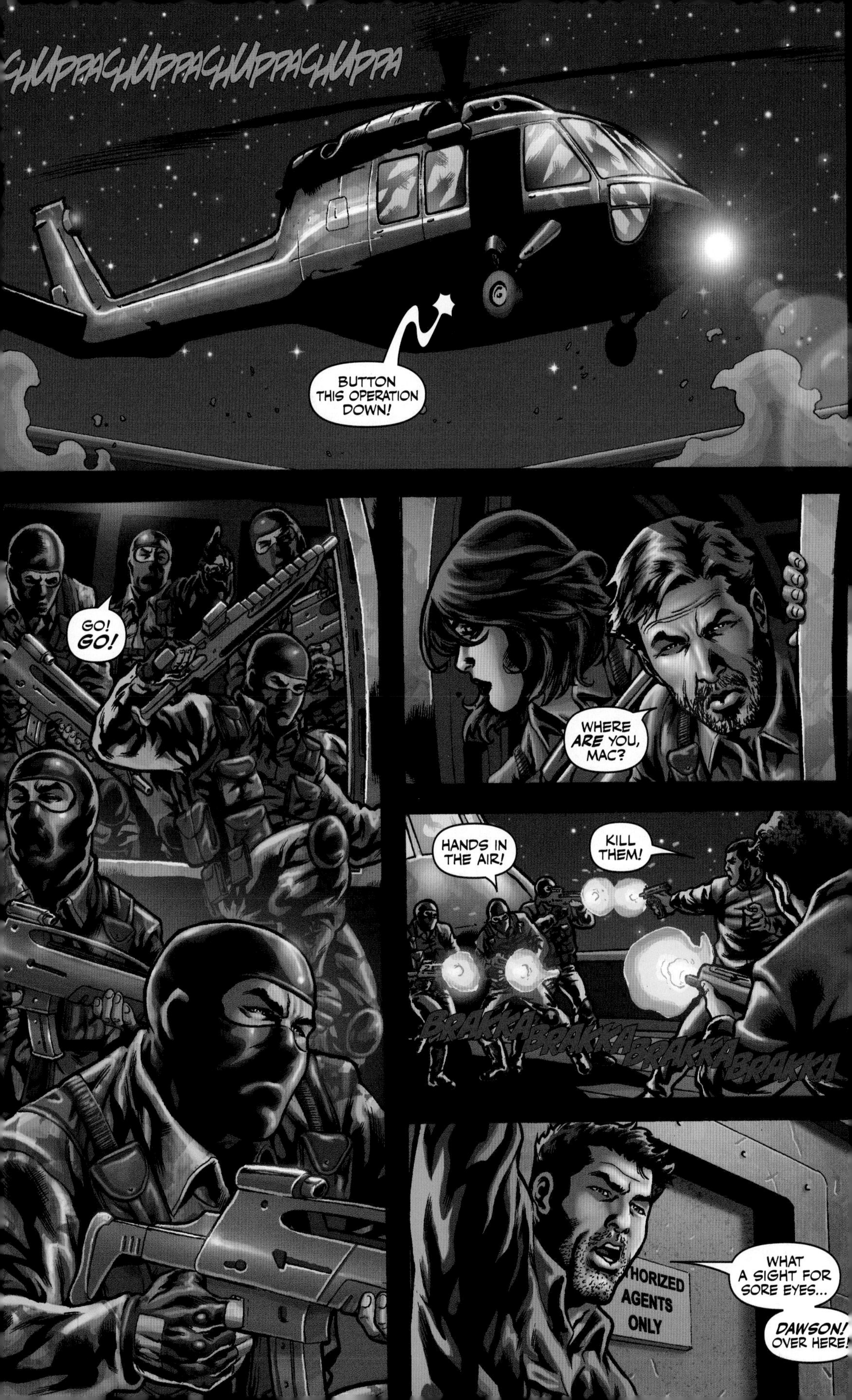
CHUPPACHUPPACHUPPACHUPPA
BUTTON THIS OPERATION DOWN!
GO! GO!
WHERE ARE YOU, MAC?
HANDS IN THE AIR!
KILL THEM!
BRAKKA BRAKKA BRAKKA BRAKKA
THORIZED AGENTS ONLY
WHAT A SIGHT FOR SORE EYES...
DAWSON! OVER HERE!

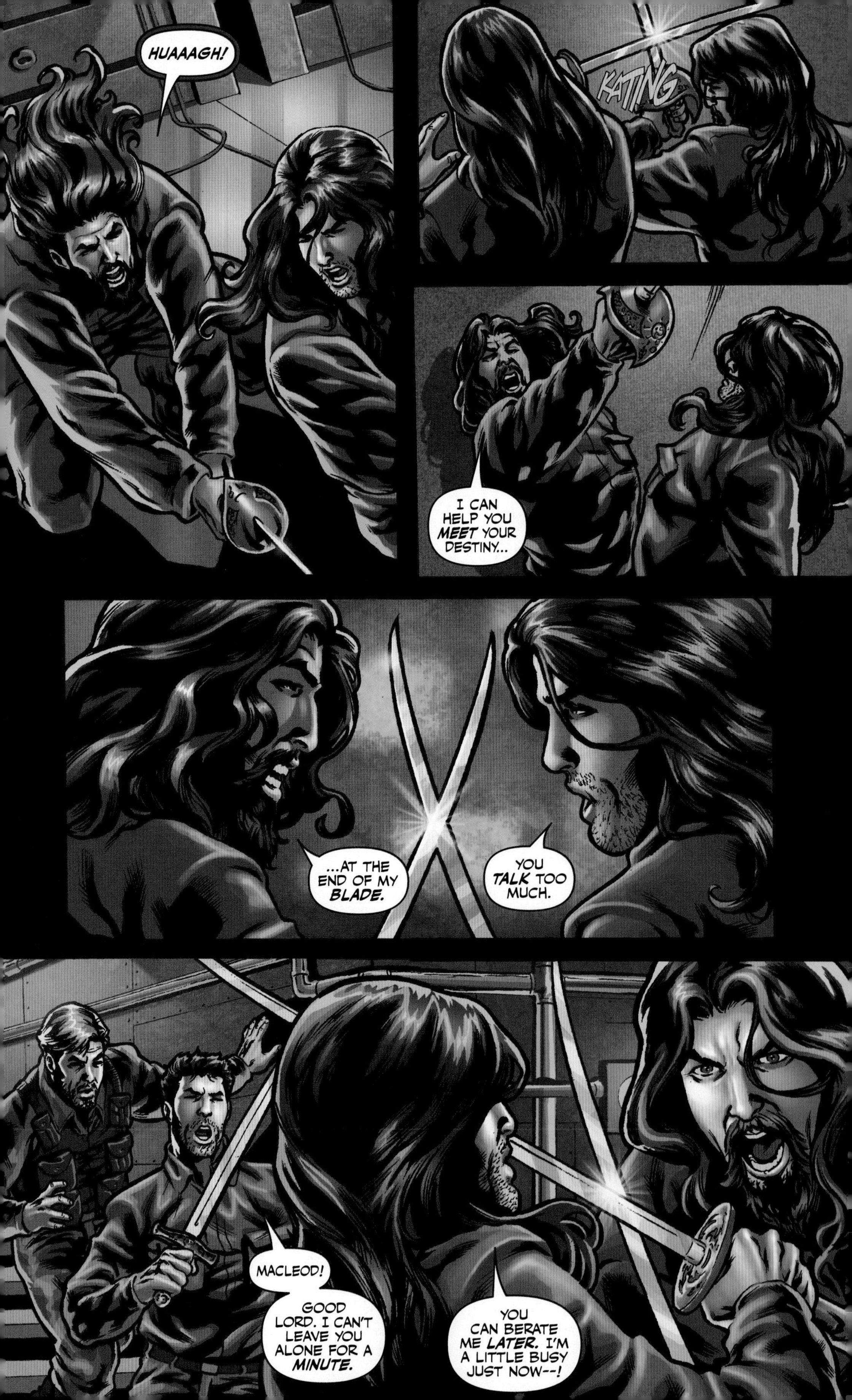
HUAAAGH!
KATING
I CAN HELP YOU *MEET* YOUR DESTINY...
...AT THE END OF MY *BLADE.*
YOU *TALK* TOO MUCH.
MACLEOD!
GOOD LORD. I CAN'T LEAVE YOU ALONE FOR A *MINUTE.*
YOU CAN BERATE ME *LATER.* I'M A LITTLE BUSY JUST NOW--!

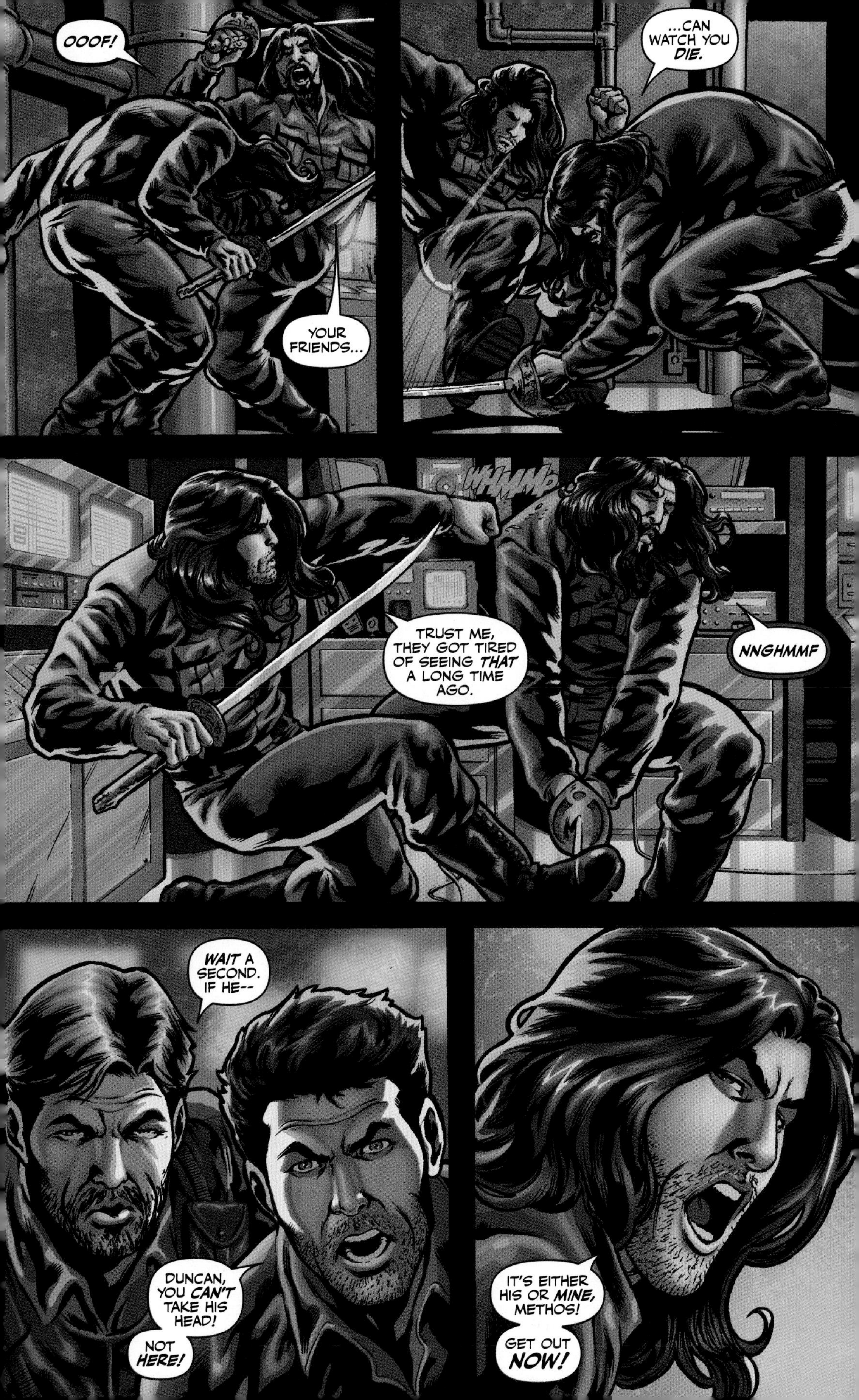
OOOF!
YOUR FRIENDS...
...CAN WATCH YOU DIE.
WHMMP
TRUST ME, THEY GOT TIRED OF SEEING THAT A LONG TIME AGO.
NNGHMMF
WAIT A SECOND. IF HE--
DUNCAN, YOU CAN'T TAKE HIS HEAD!
NOT HERE!
IT'S EITHER HIS OR MINE, METHOS!
GET OUT NOW!

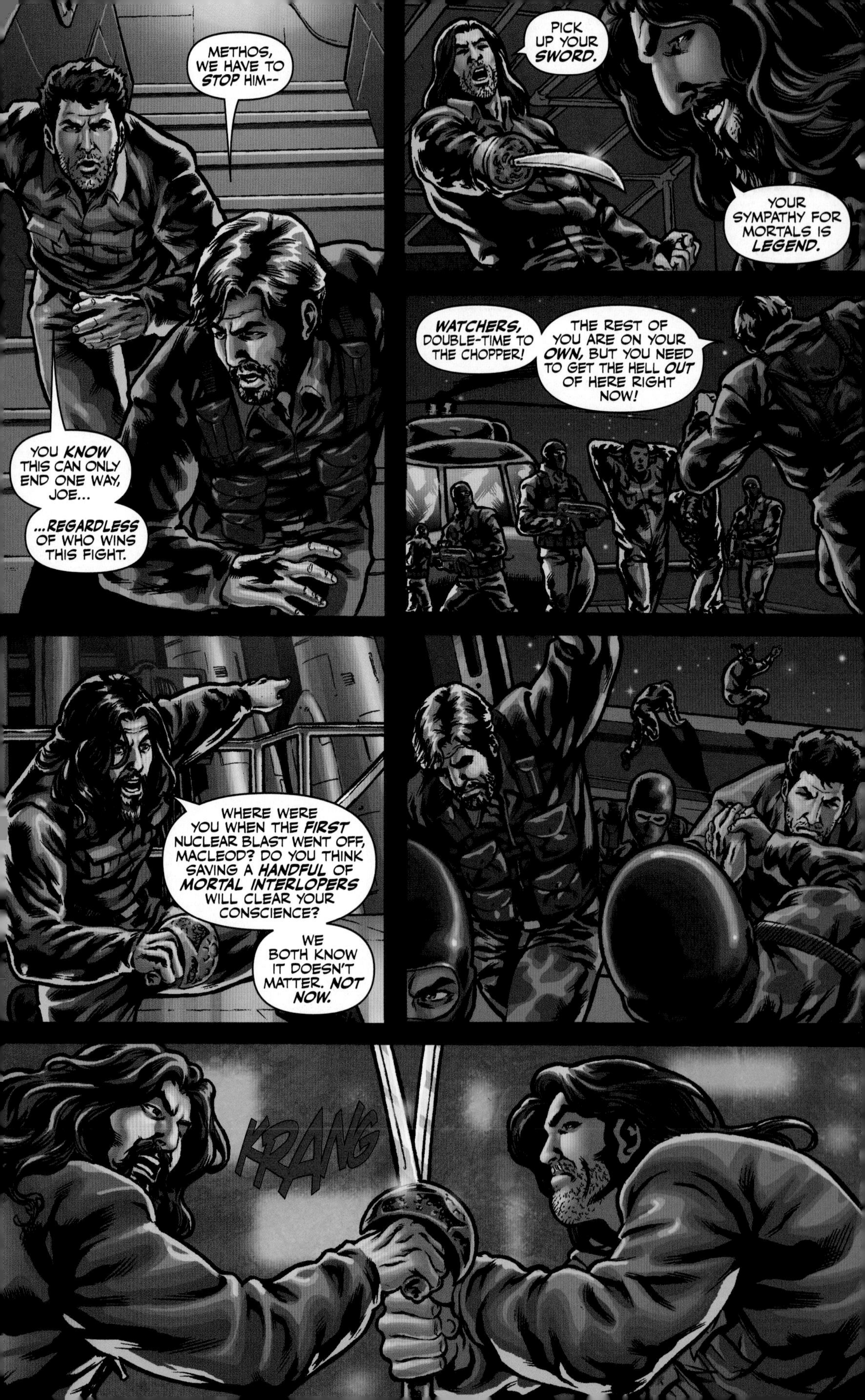
METHOS, WE HAVE TO *STOP* HIM--
YOU *KNOW* THIS CAN ONLY END ONE WAY, JOE...
...*REGARDLESS* OF WHO WINS THIS FIGHT.
PICK UP YOUR *SWORD.*
YOUR SYMPATHY FOR MORTALS IS *LEGEND.*
WATCHERS, DOUBLE-TIME TO THE CHOPPER!
THE REST OF YOU ARE ON YOUR *OWN,* BUT YOU NEED TO GET THE HELL *OUT* OF HERE RIGHT NOW!
WHERE WERE YOU WHEN THE *FIRST* NUCLEAR BLAST WENT OFF, MACLEOD? DO YOU THINK SAVING A *HANDFUL* OF *MORTAL INTERLOPERS* WILL CLEAR YOUR CONSCIENCE?
WE BOTH KNOW IT DOESN'T MATTER. *NOT NOW.*
KRANG

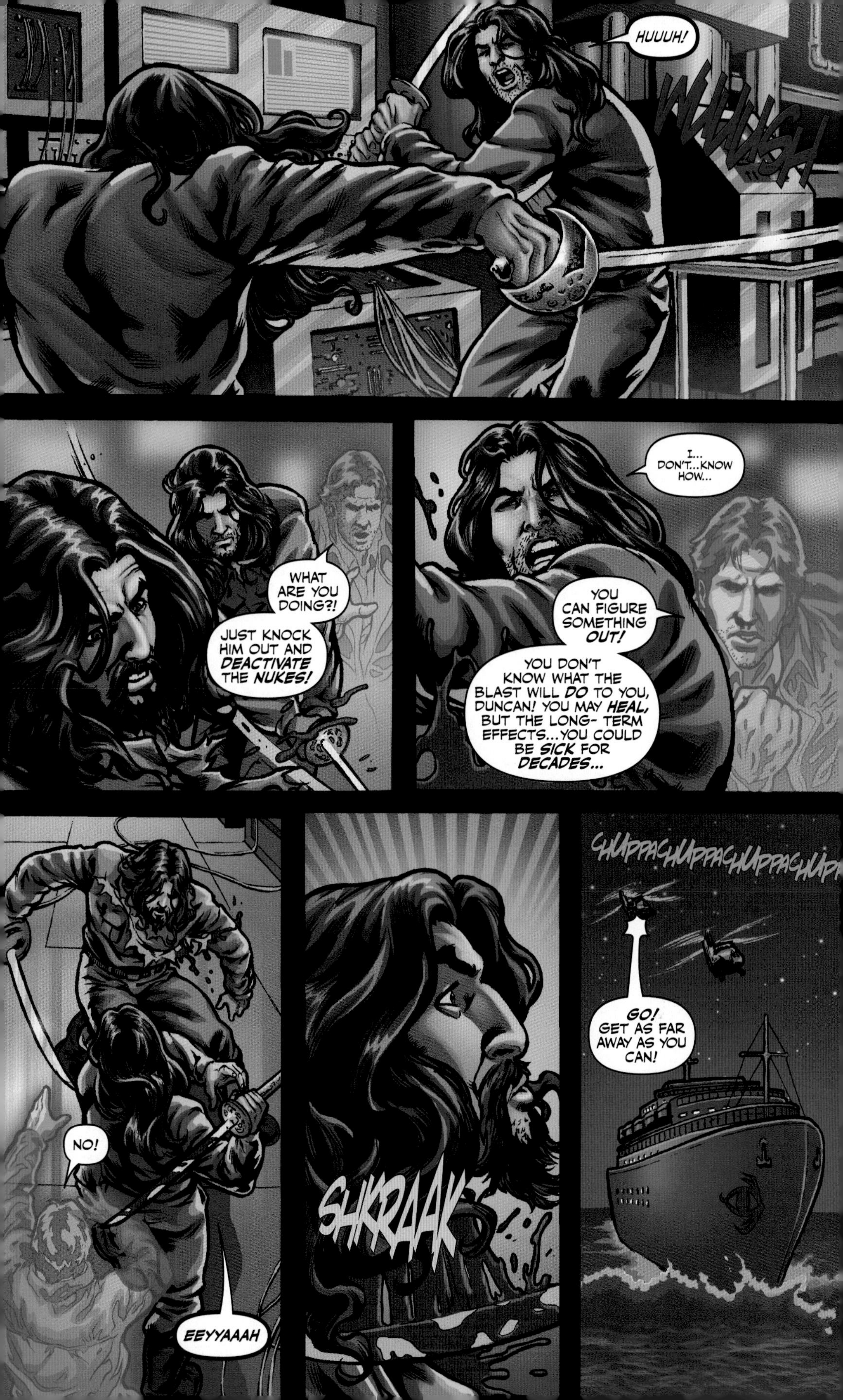
HUUUH!
WUUUSH
WHAT ARE YOU DOING?!
JUST KNOCK HIM OUT AND DEACTIVATE THE NUKES!
I... DON'T...KNOW HOW...
YOU CAN FIGURE SOMETHING OUT!
YOU DON'T KNOW WHAT THE BLAST WILL DO TO YOU, DUNCAN! YOU MAY HEAL, BUT THE LONG- TERM EFFECTS...YOU COULD BE SICK FOR DECADES...
NO!
EEYYAAAH
SHKRAAK
CHUPPACHUPPACHUPPACHUPP
GO! GET AS FAR AWAY AS YOU CAN!

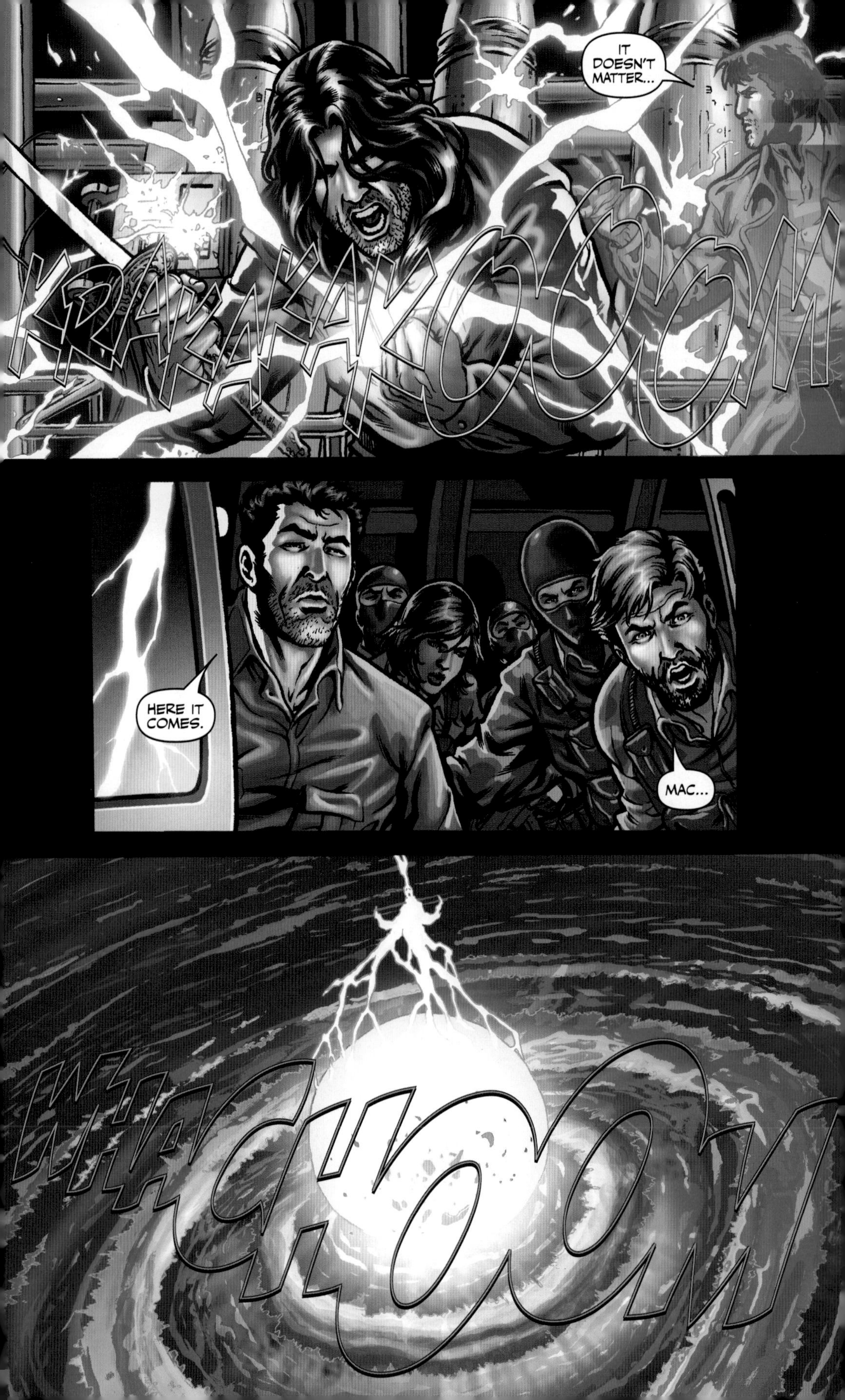
IT DOESN'T MATTER...
HERE IT COMES.
MAC...

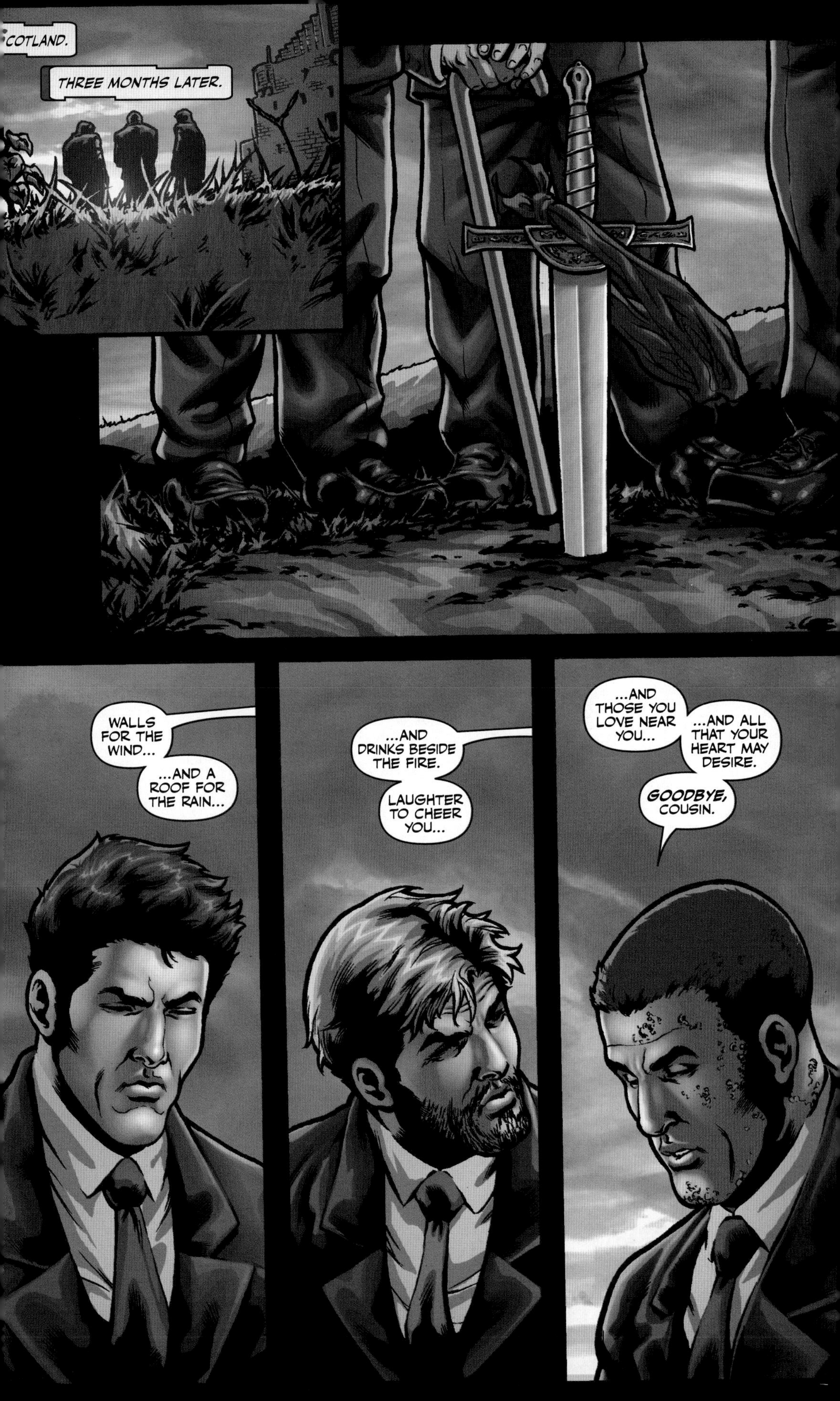
COTLAND.
THREE MONTHS LATER.
WALLS FOR THE WIND...
...AND A ROOF FOR THE RAIN...
...AND DRINKS BESIDE THE FIRE.
LAUGHTER TO CHEER YOU...
...AND THOSE YOU LOVE NEAR YOU...
...AND ALL THAT YOUR HEART MAY DESIRE.
GOODBYE, COUSIN.

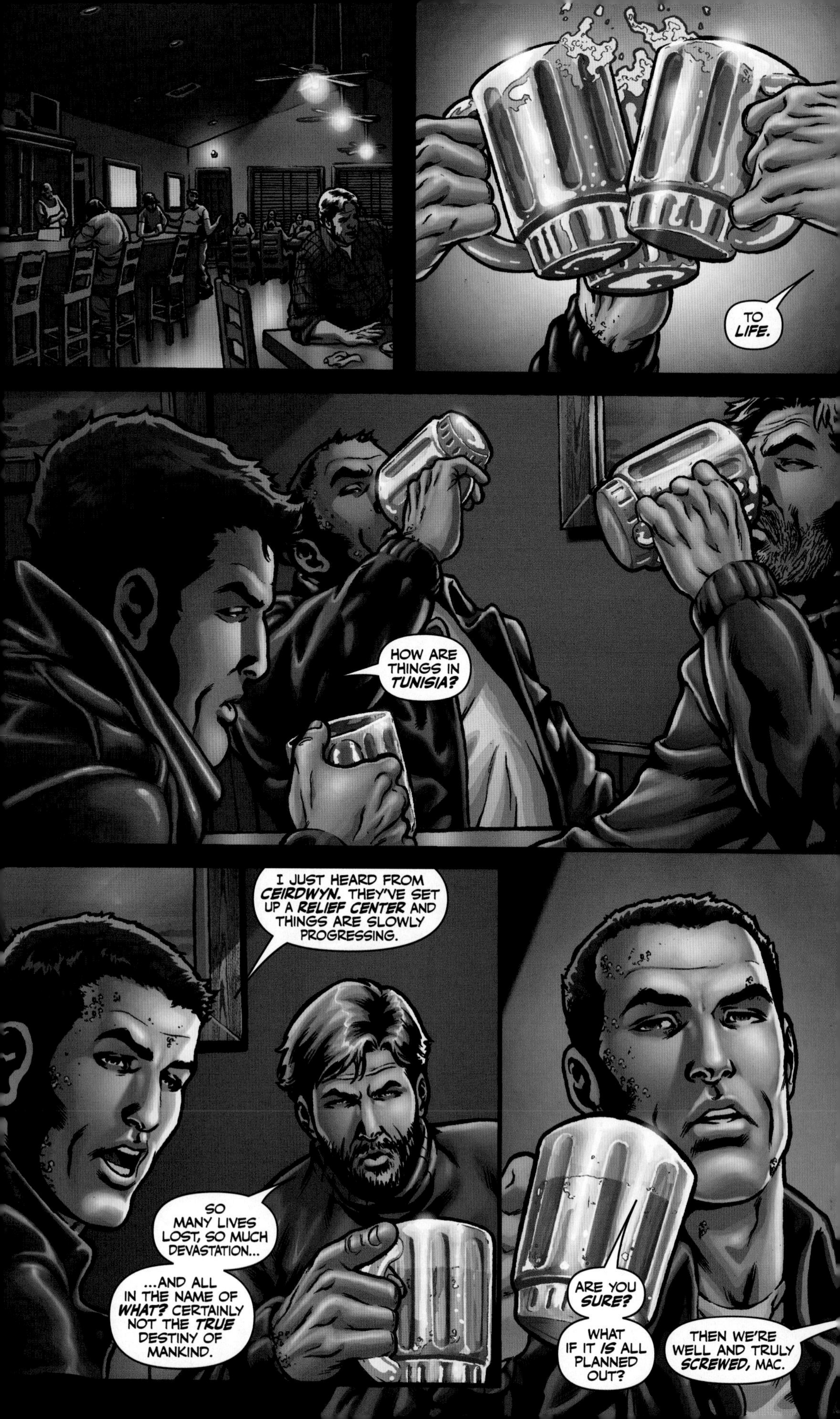
TO LIFE.
HOW ARE THINGS IN TUNISIA?
I JUST HEARD FROM CEIRDWYN. THEY'VE SET UP A RELIEF CENTER AND THINGS ARE SLOWLY PROGRESSING.
SO MANY LIVES LOST, SO MUCH DEVASTATION...
...AND ALL IN THE NAME OF WHAT? CERTAINLY NOT THE TRUE DESTINY OF MANKIND.
ARE YOU SURE?
WHAT IF IT IS ALL PLANNED OUT?
THEN WE'RE WELL AND TRULY SCREWED, MAC.

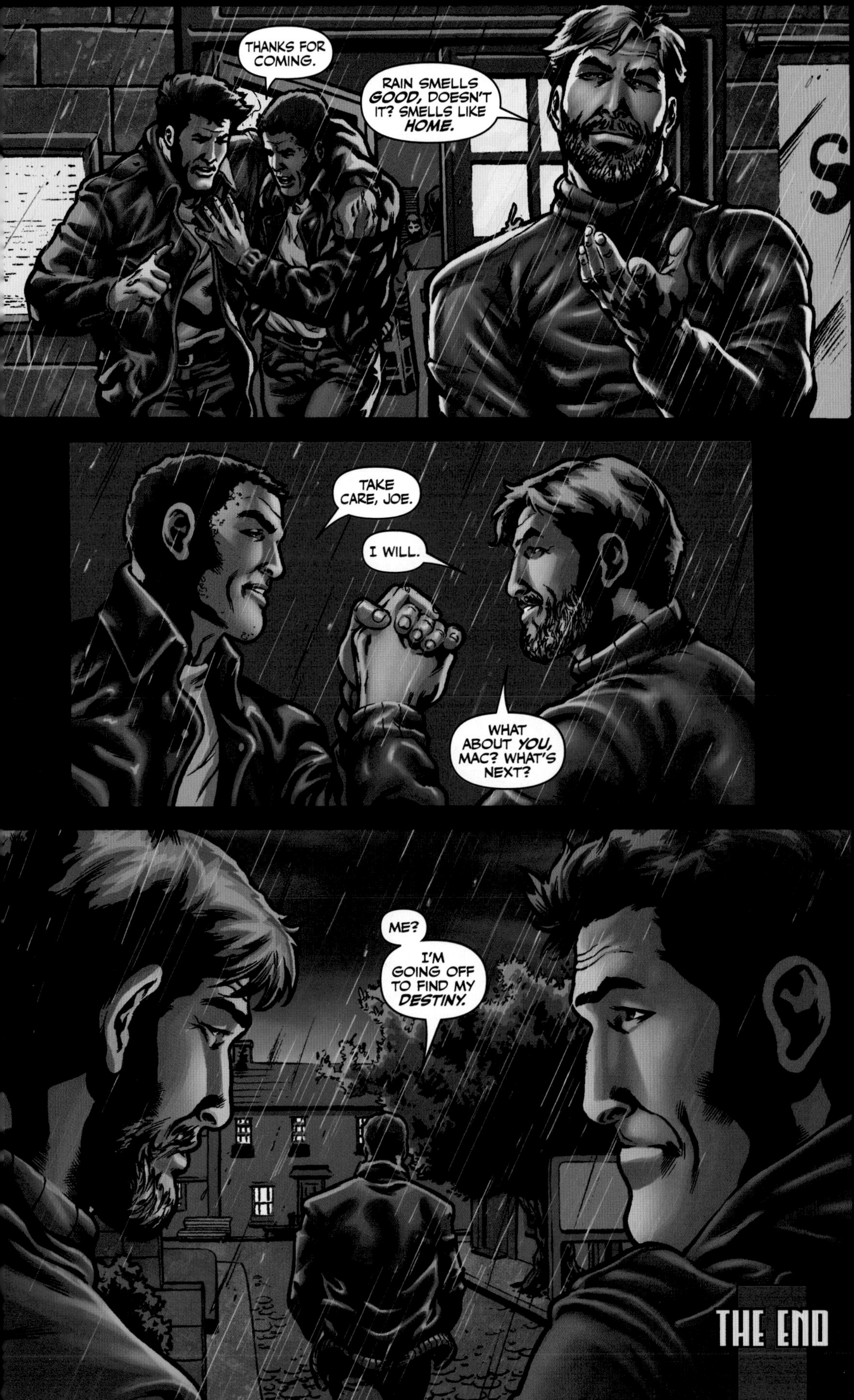
THANKS FOR COMING.
RAIN SMELLS GOOD, DOESN'T IT? SMELLS LIKE HOME.
TAKE CARE, JOE.
I WILL.
WHAT ABOUT YOU, MAC? WHAT'S NEXT?
ME?
I'M GOING OFF TO FIND MY DESTINY.
THE END

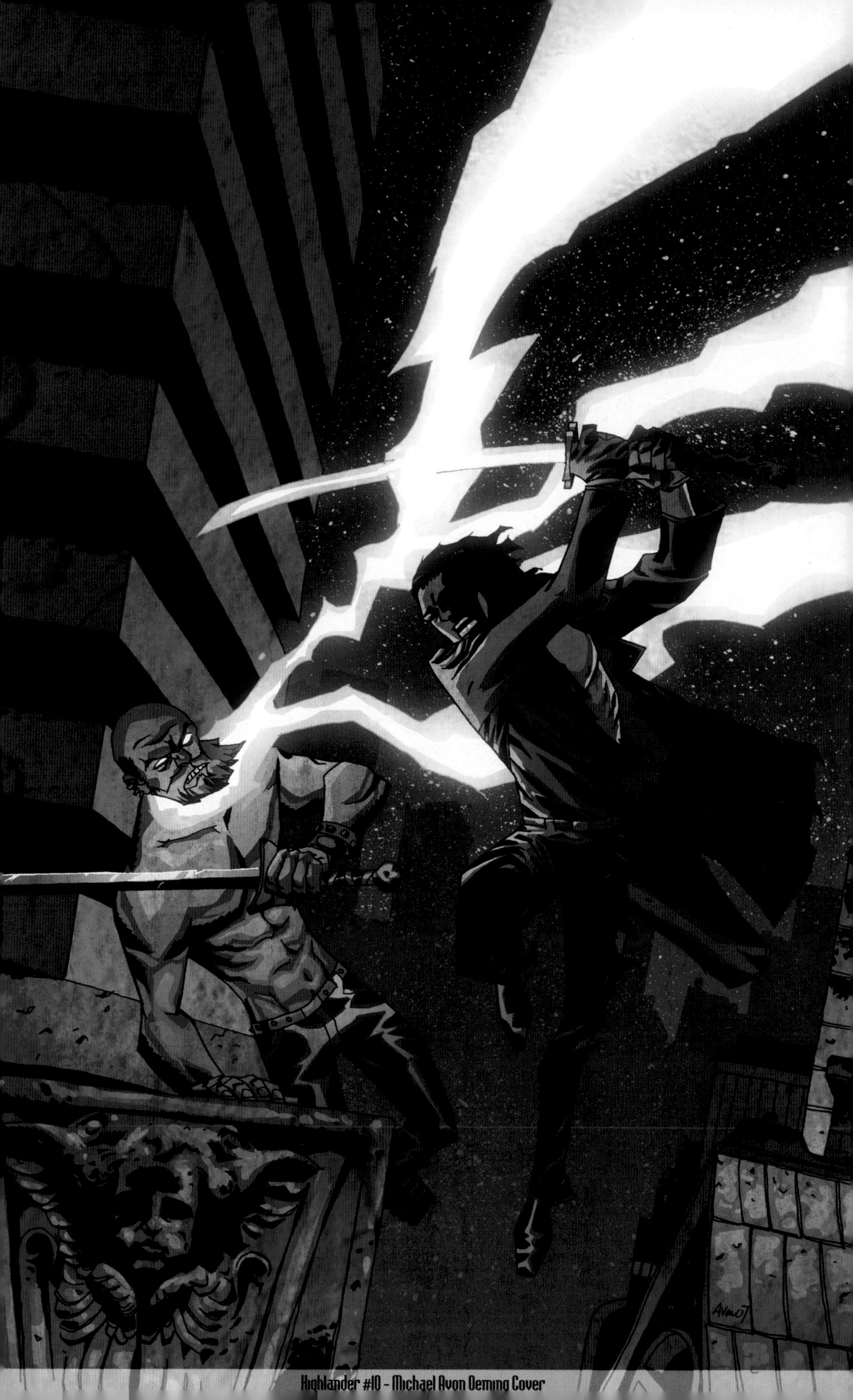
AVM07

Highlander #10 - Michael Avon Oeming Cover

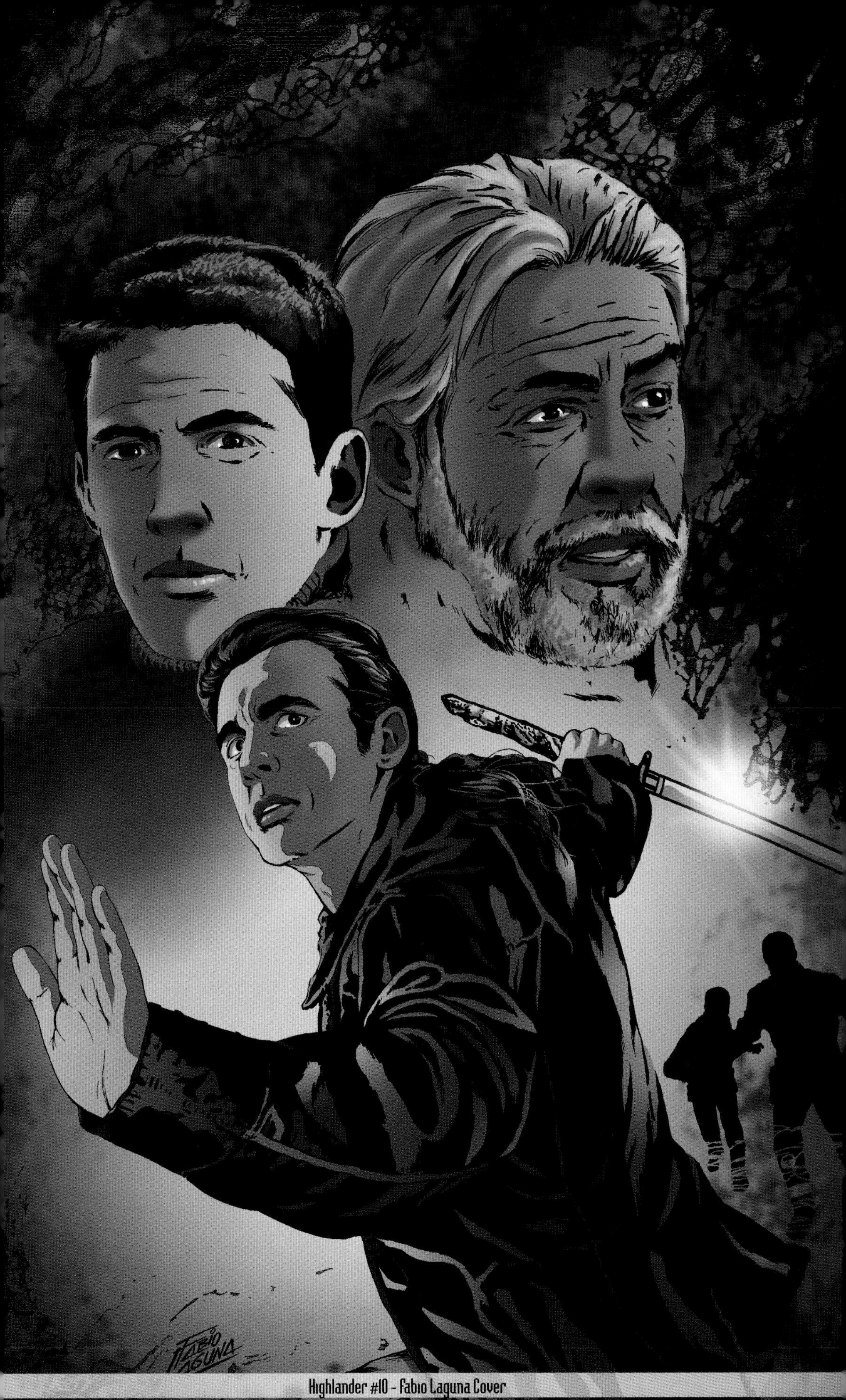
FABIO LAGUNA
Highlander #10 - Fabio Laguna Cover

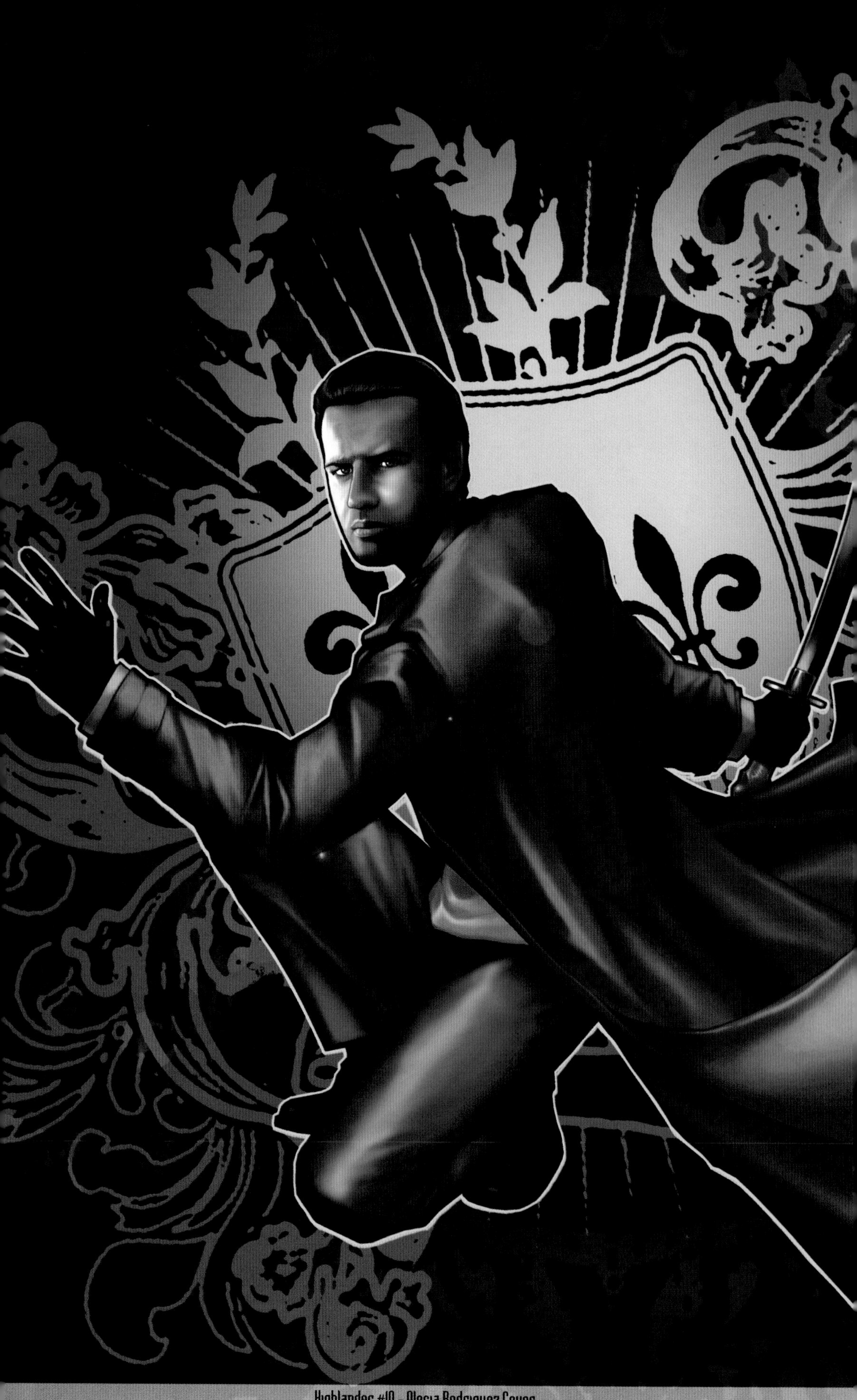

Highlander #10 - Alecia Rodriguez Cover

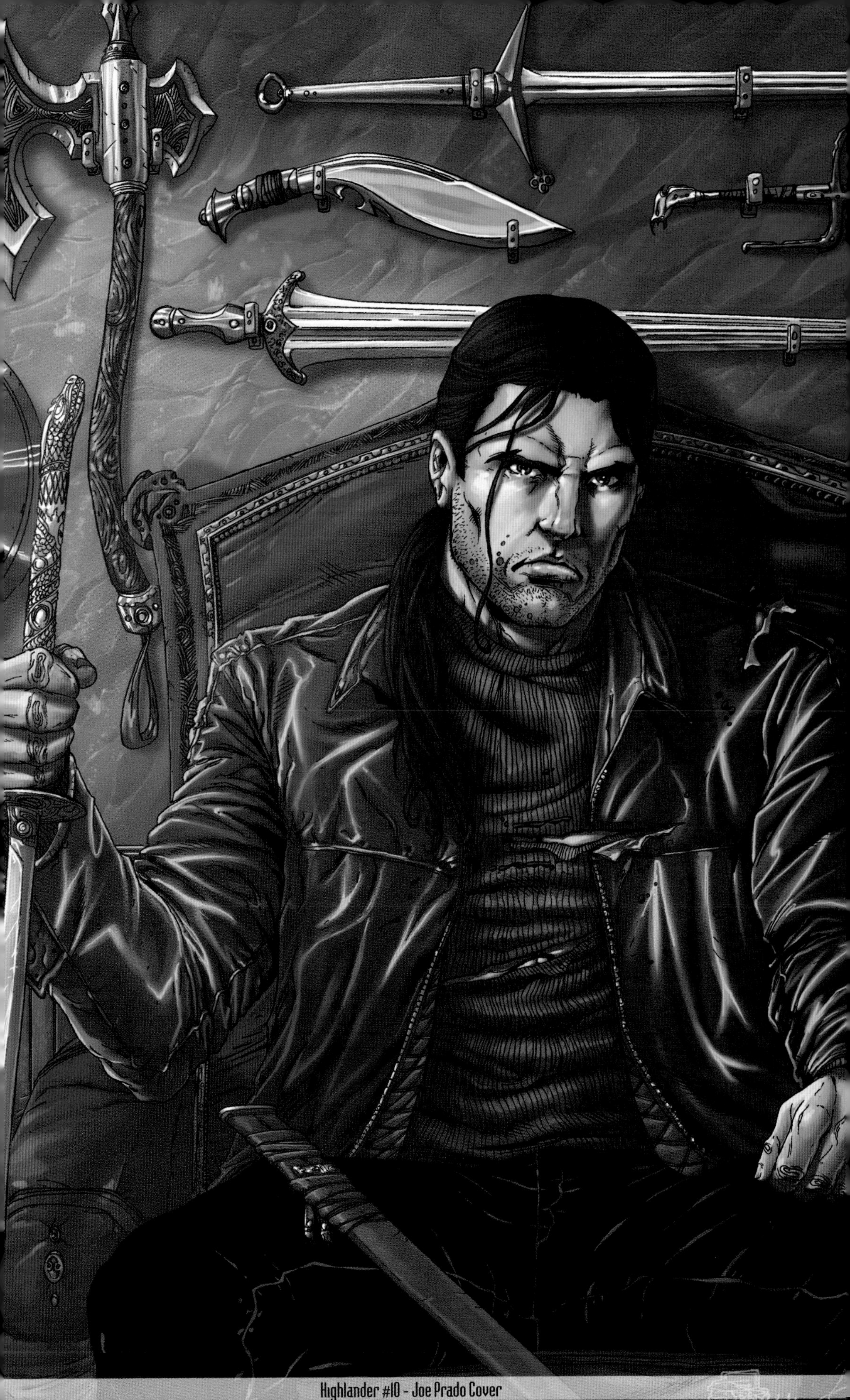

Highlander #10 - Joe Prado Cover

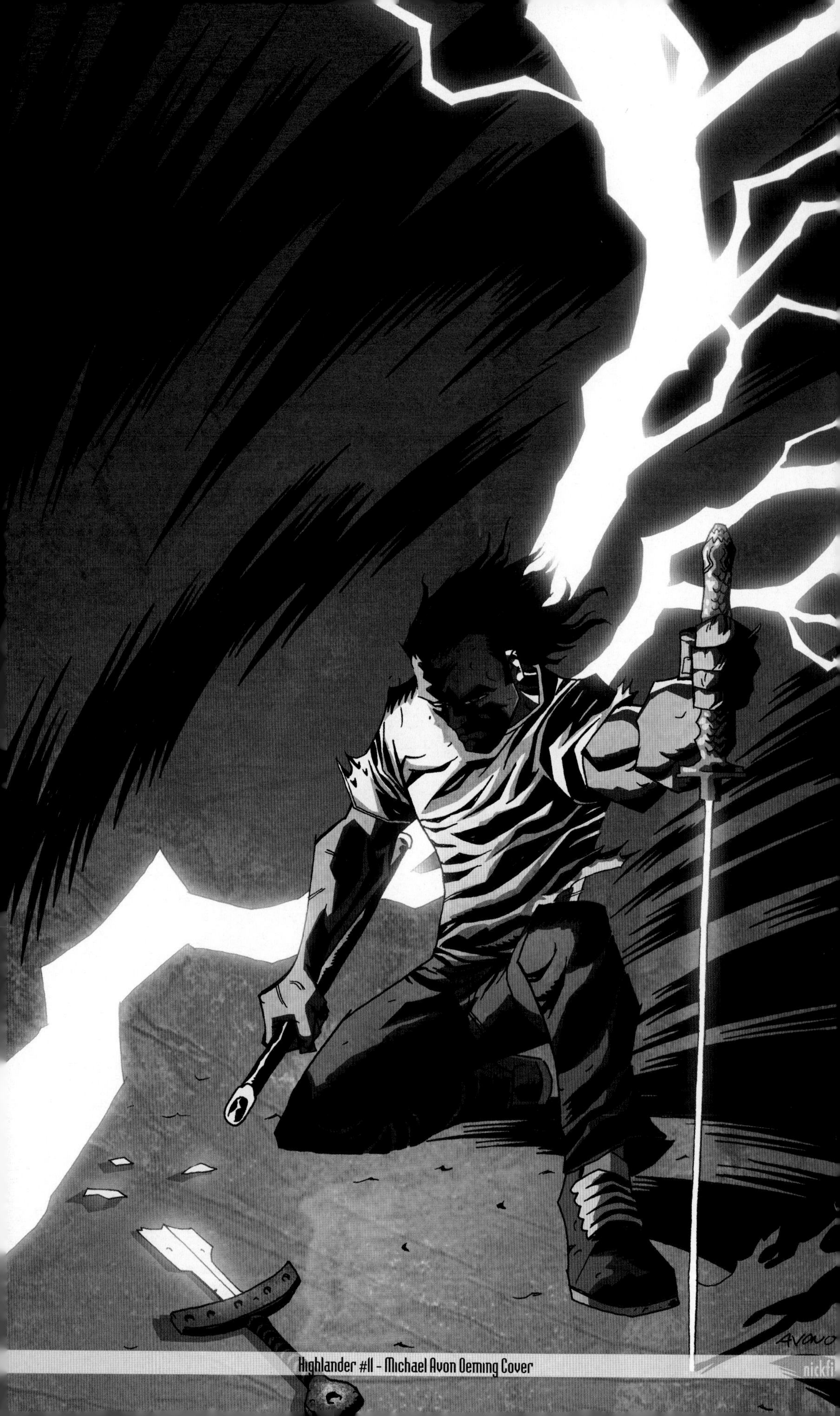

Highlander #11 - Michael Avon Oeming Cover

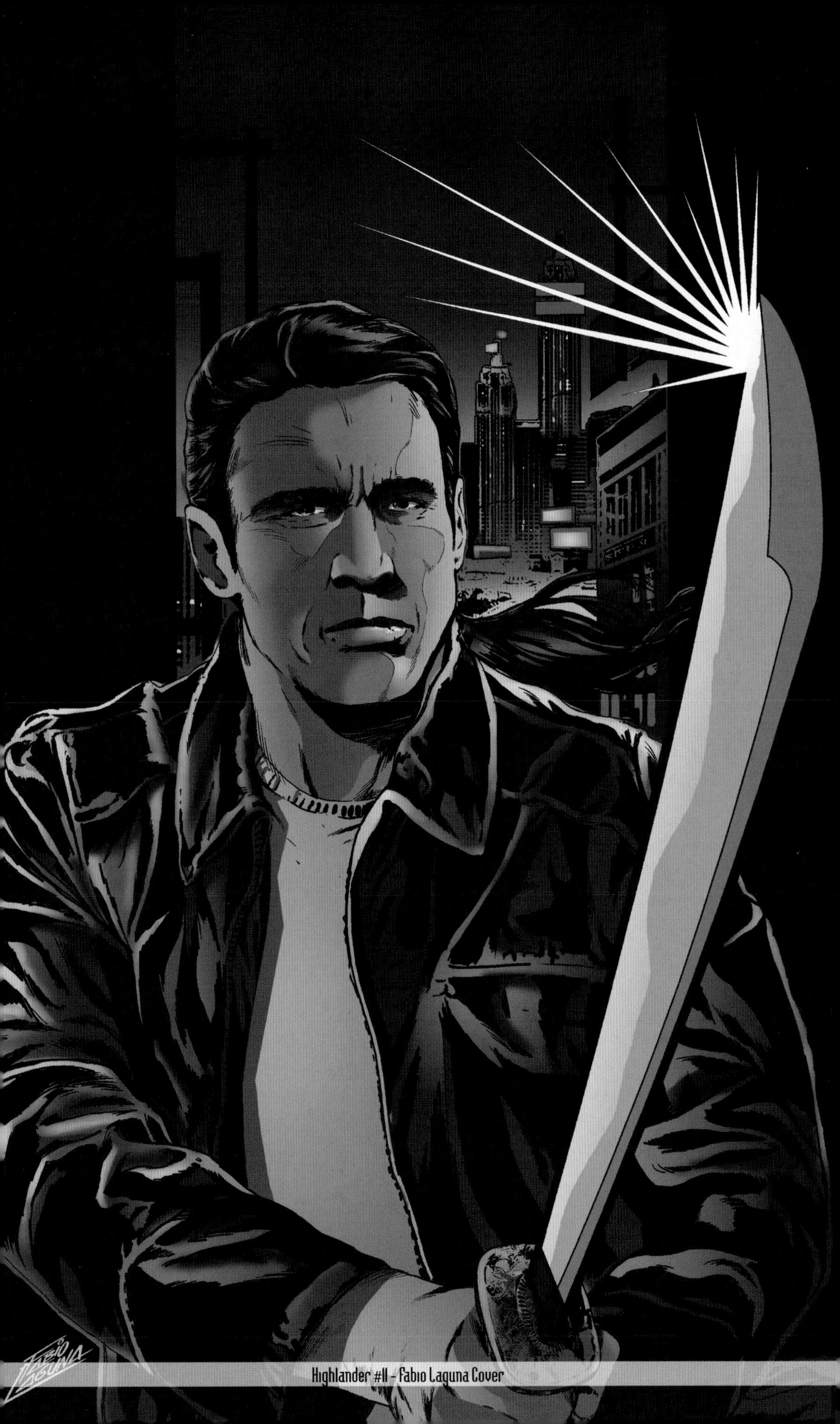
FABIO LAGUNA
Highlander #11 - Fabio Laguna Cover

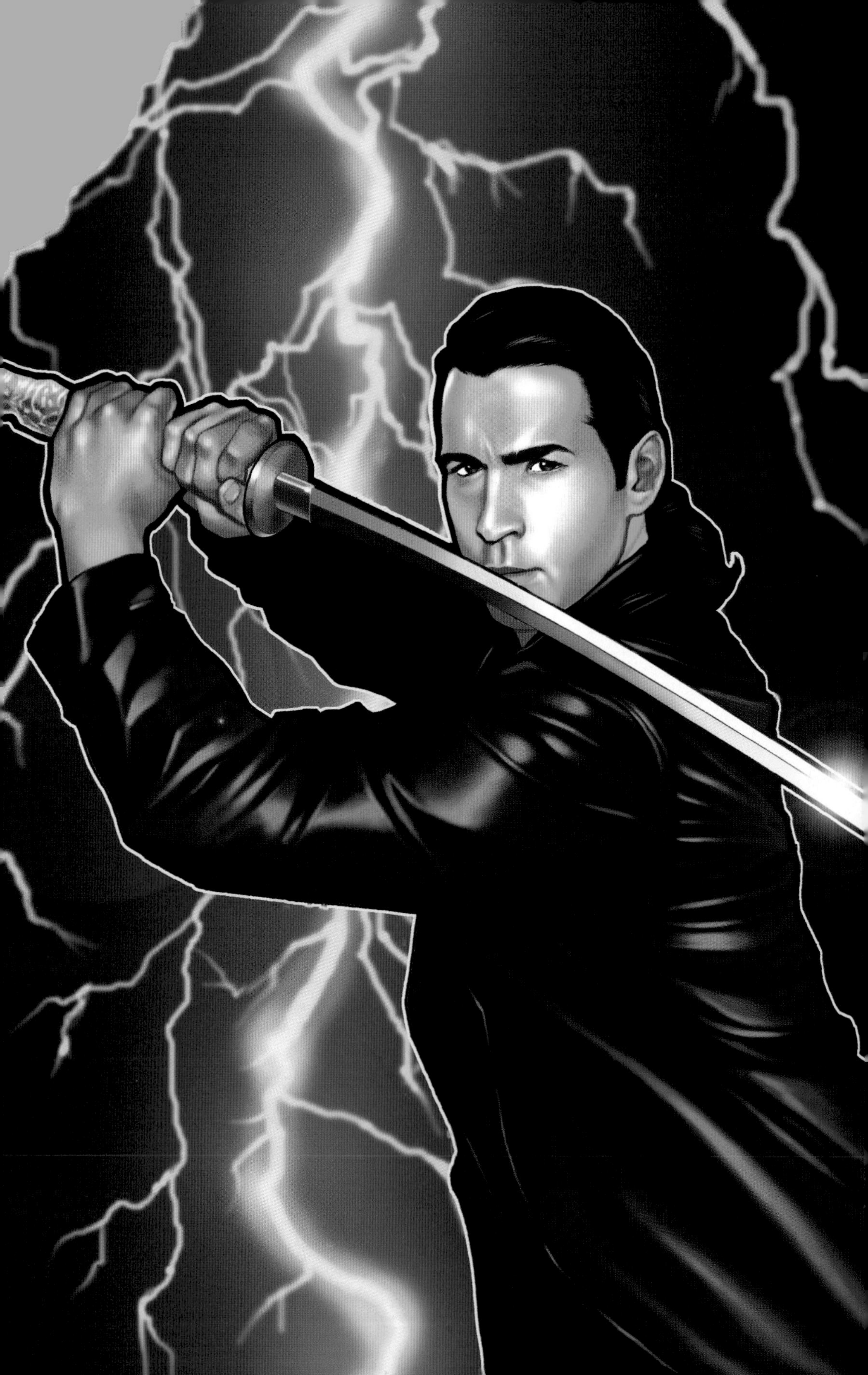

Highlander #11 - Alecia Rodriguez Cover

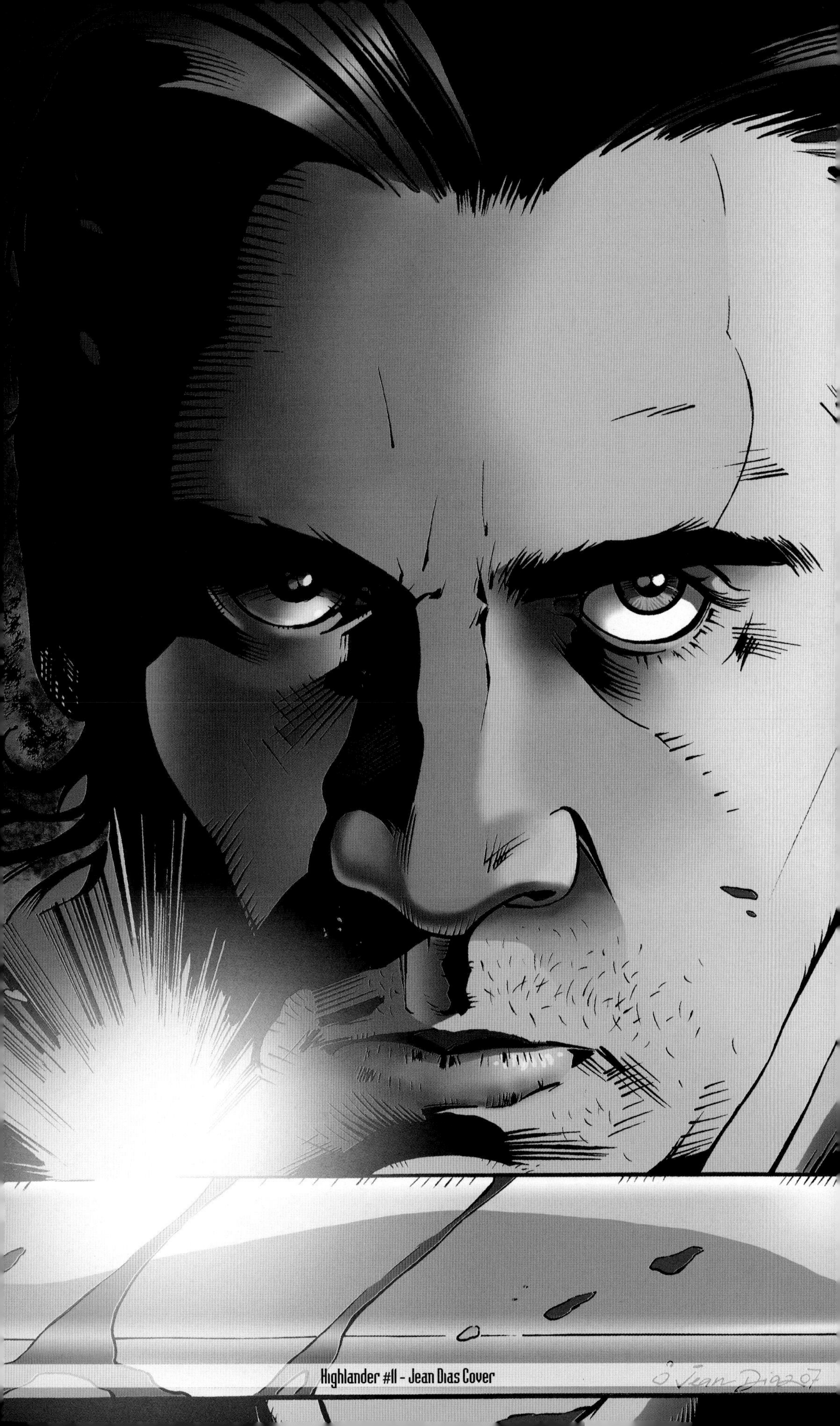

Highlander #11 - Jean Dias Cover

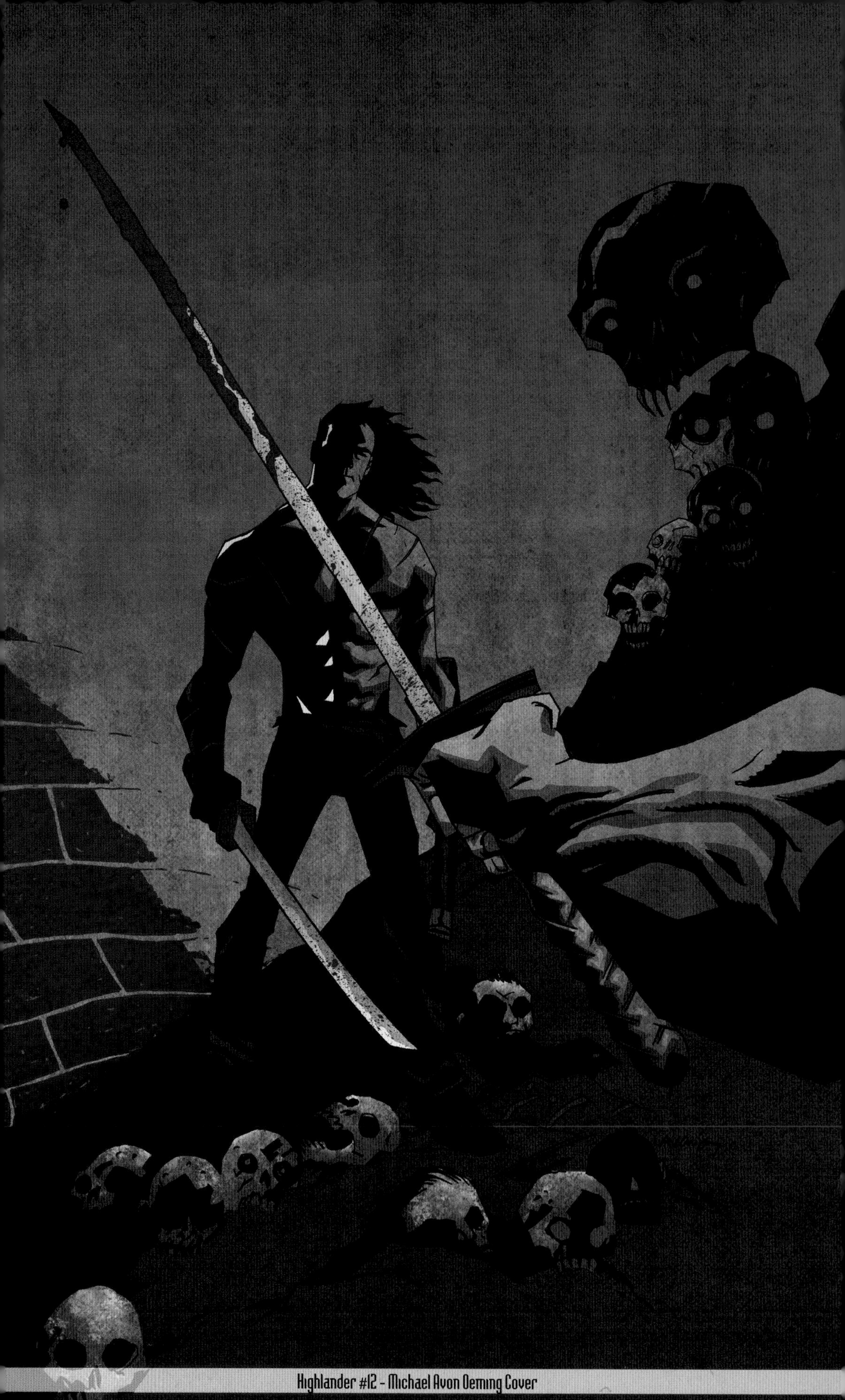

Highlander #12 - Michael Avon Oeming Cover

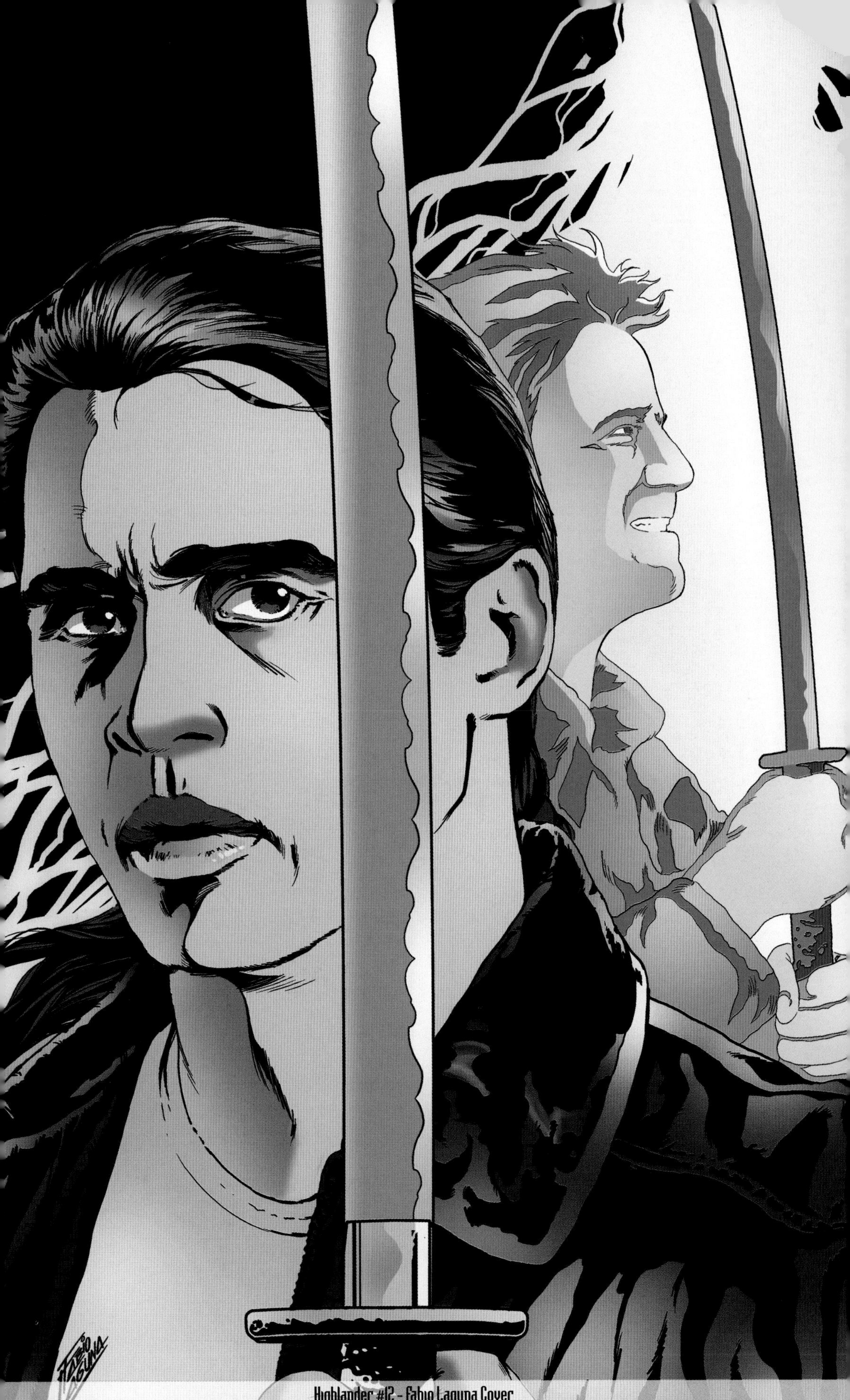

Highlander #12 - Fabio Laguna Cover

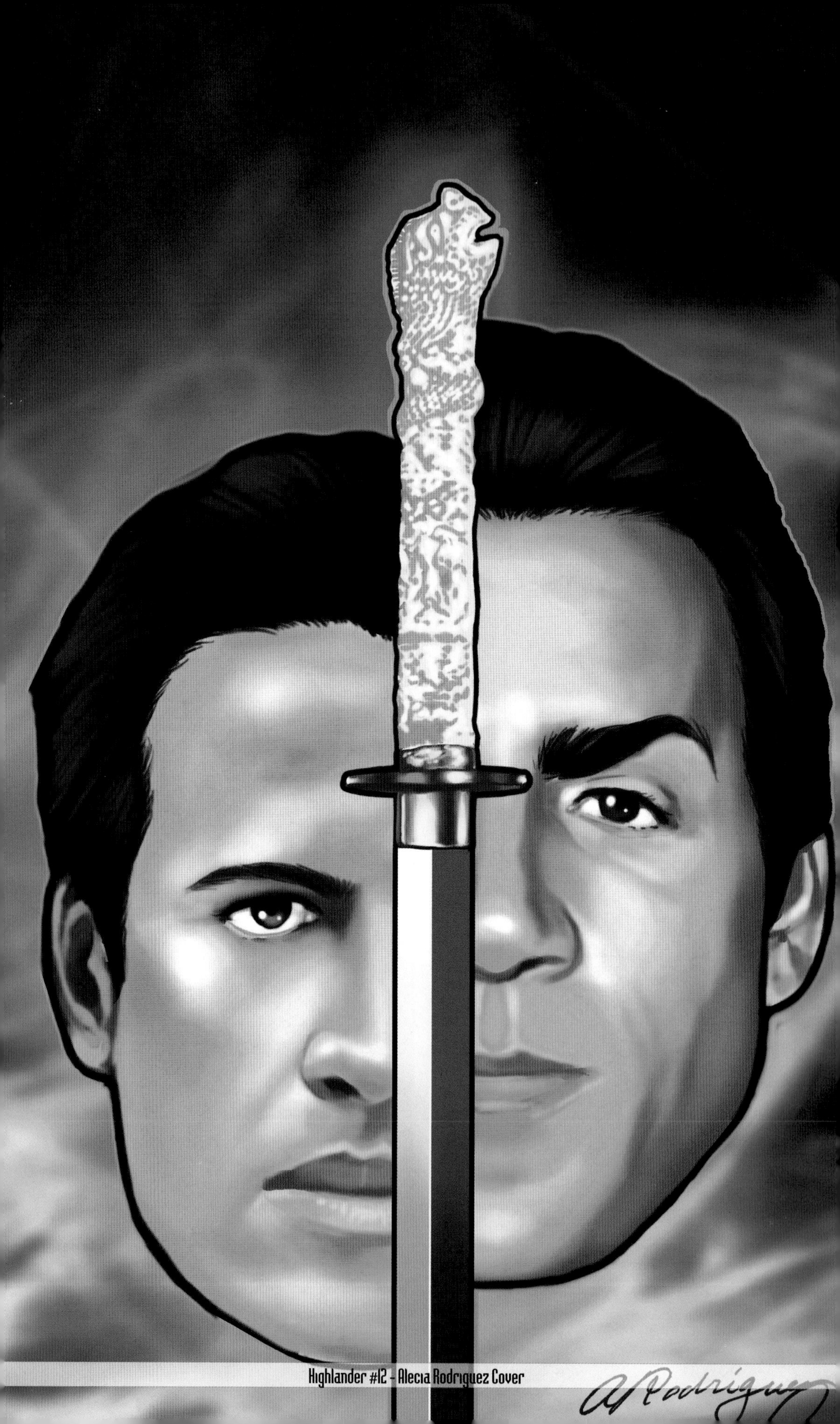
ARodriguez

Highlander #12 - Alecia Rodriguez Cover

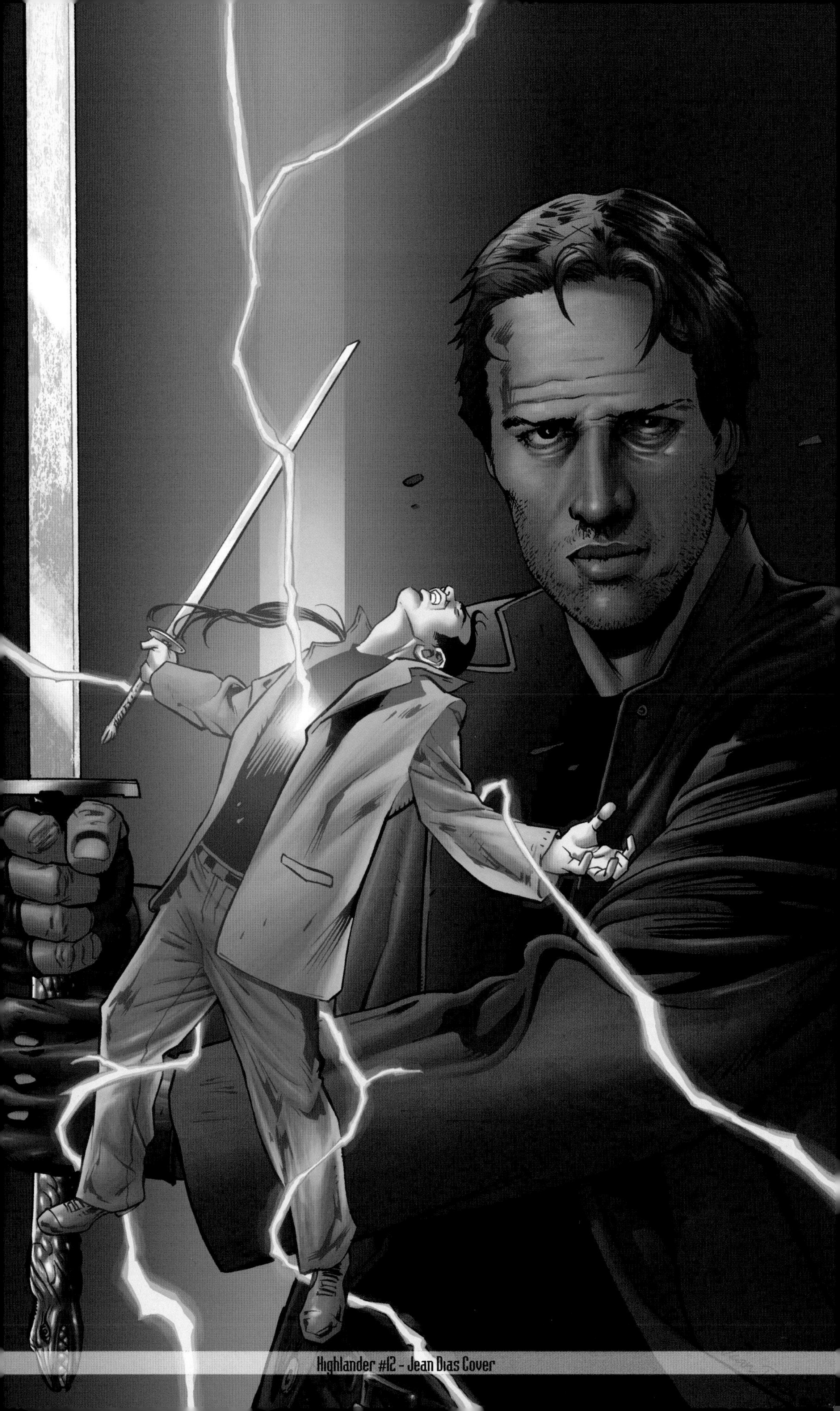
Highlander #12 - Jean Dias Cover

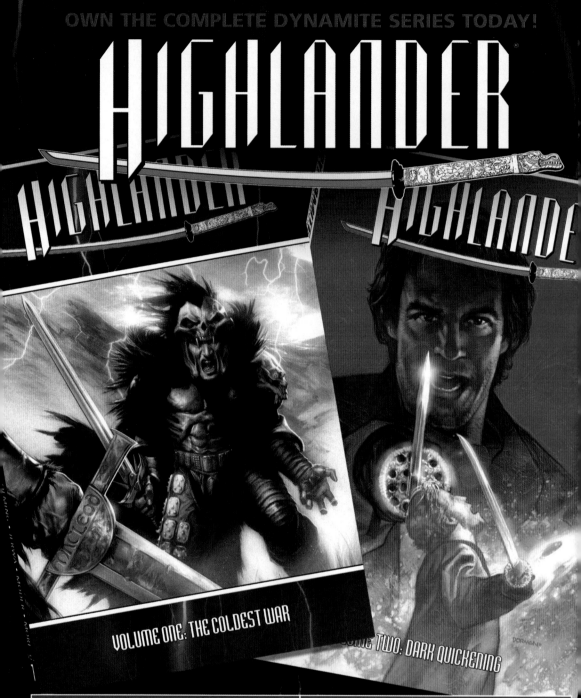